Gold Mining in Gilpin County Colorado

Compiled by Samuel Cushman and J.P. Waterman

with an introduction by Kerby Jackson

This work contains material that was originally published by
the United States Geological Survey in 1876.

This publication was created and published for the public benefit,
utilizing public funding and is within the Public Domain.

This edition is reprinted for educational purposes
and in accordance with all applicable Federal Laws.

Introduction Copyright 2014 by Kerby Jackson

Introduction

It has been nearly 140 years years since the partnership of Cushman and Waterman released it's important publication "The Gold Mines of Gilpin County, Colorado". First released in 1876, this important volume has now been out of print and has been unavailable to the mining community since those days, with the exception of expensive original collector's copies and poorly produced digital editions.

It has often been said that "*gold is where you find it*", but even beginning prospectors understand that their chances for finding something of value in the earth or in the streams of the Golden West are dramatically increased by going back to those places where gold and other minerals were once mined by our forerunners. Despite this, much of the contemporary information on local mining history that is currently available is mostly a result of mere local folklore and persistent rumors of major strikes, the details and facts of which, have long been distorted. Long gone are the old timers and with them, the days of first hand knowledge of the mines of the area and how they operated. Also long gone are most of their notes, their assay reports, their mine maps and personal scrapbooks, along with most of the surveys and reports that were performed for them by private and government geologists. Even published books such as this one are often retired to the local landfill or backyard burn pile by the descendents of those old timers and disappear at an alarming rate. Despite the fact that we live in the so-called "Information Age" where information is supposedly only the push of a button on a keyboard away, true insight into mining properties remains illusive and hard to come by, even to those of us who seek out this sort of information as if our lives depend upon it. Without this type of information readily available to the average independent miner, there is little hope that our metal mining industry will ever recover.

This important volume and others like it, are being presented in their entirety again, in the hope that the average prospector will no longer stumble through the overgrown hills and the tailing strewn creeks without being well informed enough to have a chance to succeed at his ventures.

                                                          Kerby Jackson
                                                          Josephine County, Oregon
                                                          June 2014

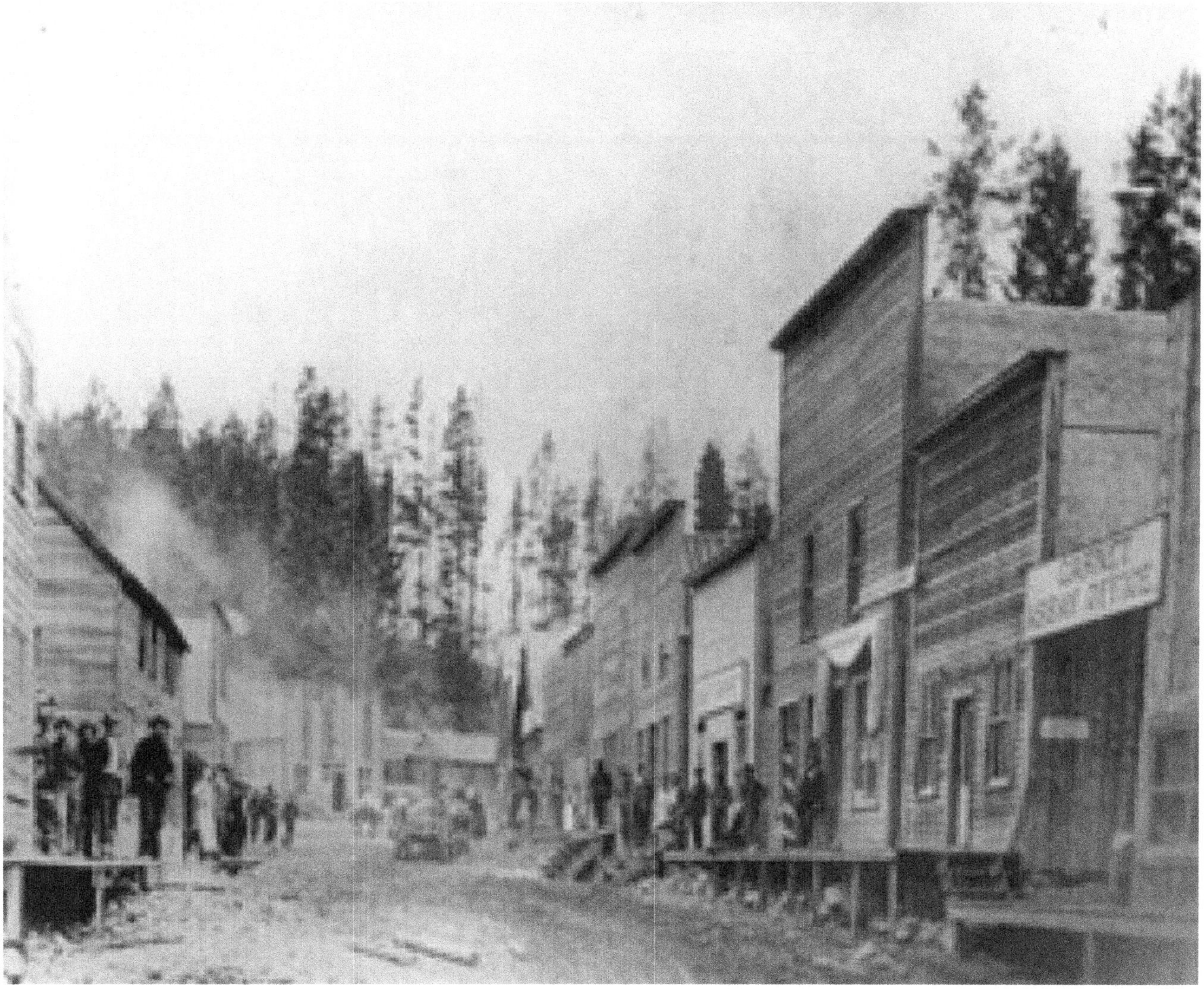

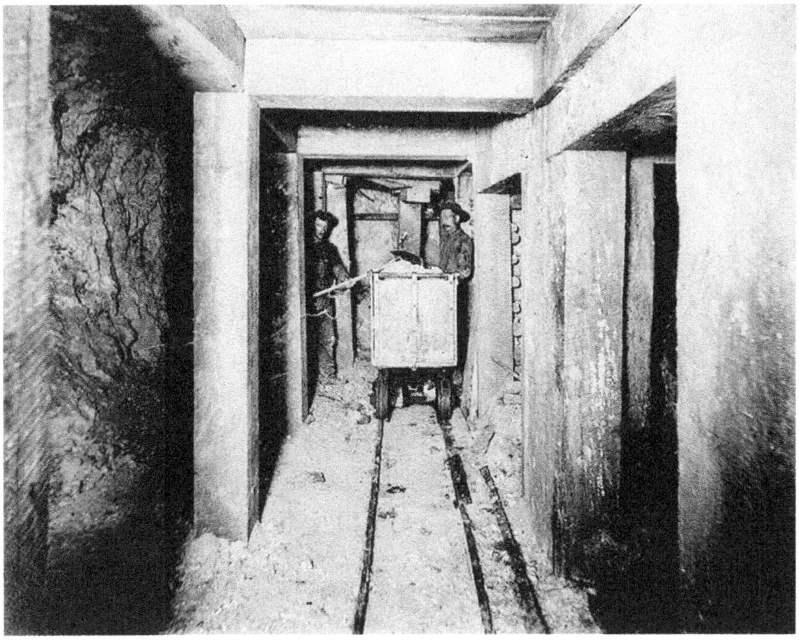

THE GOLD MINES

—OF—

GILPIN COUNTY,

COLORADO.

HISTORICAL.

The year 1857 was, financially, a bad one. Thousands were in a wilderness of debt, waiting for a Moses, and dreaming of a promised land. Stray items in the Western and Southern newspapers informed the world, that gold had been found on the South Platte and its tributaries. The news was indefinite, and proof of its correctness rested upon such doubtful authority as returned trappers, Indian traders and Cherokees. Yet, with the brilliant success of California gold mining to give them hope, and urged to new fields by disaster or stagnation at home, there was not wanting a multitude of enterprising and adventurous men, ready to make another stride westward.

By some unknown means the news had reached far away Georgia, and early in 1858,

W. GREEN RUSSELL.

and his brother, "Doc" Russell, with a party of nine men, started on a two-thousand-mile journey for the mouth of Cherry Creek, then known only as a favorite winter camp of the Indians, on the old Cherokee trail, and an occasional camping place of government trains traversing from Fort Laramie to the southern forts. Unlike the mass of gold-seekers that followed later, this party had learned placer

RICHARDS & CO.,

Wholesale and Retail Dealers in

BOOKS AND STATIONERY,

FINE CUTLERY, GOLD PENS,

PICTURES and PICTURE-FRAMES.

Largest assortment of Colorado Views in the Territory.

---

372 Larimer Street,   DENVER, COL.

J. S. Brown.   J. F. Brown.

J. S. BROWN & BRO.,

375 Blake St., Denver,

WHOLESALE GROCERS,

—DEALERS IN—

Liquors, Provisions,

COAL OIL AND NAILS.

GENERAL AGENTS FOR DUPONT POWDER.

J. F. Simmons, Agent,   H. J. Kruse, Agent,
     Georgetown.   Central City.

mining in their native State, and in California. Entering the valley by the way of Cherry Creek, early in June, they prospected on all the tributaries of the Platte from Plum Creek to Cache-a-la-Poudre. The most promising diggings were found on a dry gulch six miles above Denver, which they called Montana Diggings. Here they washed about sixty dollars—enough to satisfy them that more and better diggings could be found—when a part of their number returned to the Missouri River for supplies, carrying the news, and the proof of the discovery.

Returning by the Platte route, Russell and his friends met on their way out from Plattsmouth, quite a large party, which had started entirely independent of the Georgia party. Among these were D. C. Oaks, A. H. Barker and Joseph Harper. Soon after the arrival of the Plattsmouth party, some of their number returned to "the river" for additional supplies. Their report confirming that of Russell, numerous small parties from several Western States started for what they called the Pike's Peak gold region; so that not less than three hundred white men, to say nothing of representatives of half a dozen Indian tribes, wintered in the Platte valley, making headquarters on the present site of West Denver, then called Auraria. Diggings were found on Clear Creek below Golden, and called Arapahoe. These, with the Montana Diggings, were worked with moderate success through the winter of 1859.

These pioneers came with no lofty ideas of forming a new State, but during the winter the American instinct cropped out in the survey of a town-site, the organization of a town company, the carving out of a new county in Kansas to be called Arapahoe, and the election and sending of a Delegate to Congress with instructions to get the new gold country set off from Kansas as a new Territory.

In the Spring of 1859, the tide of immigration set in early and strong, but ebbed as soon. Hundreds that came in and found only limited "grub diggings," were disgusted with the "great cry and little wool," and turned homeward without unloading their wagons. They were so indignant that they even refused to sell their provisions to those who chose to remain and prospect the mountains, and threatened to hang

BEST'S PHARMACY

—OPPOSITE TELLER HOUSE—

CENTRAL CITY, - COL.,

IS HEADQUARTERS FOR

DRUGS, MILL CHEMICALS

QUICKSILVER,

Paints, Oils, Glass, Brushes, Etc.

Assaying Implements and Photographic Stock.

Call or send for prices. Orders by mail promptly attended to at bottom prices.

those who had written encouraging reports. A large party returning to Plattsmouth, threatened to burn that town, alleging that the gold excitement was gotten up by the merchants there to create a demand for their goods. They reported the Pike's Peak camp as starving, and that Barker and Oaks were hung; that the headstone of the latter's grave was the shoulder-blade of a buffalo, on which the following epitaph was written:

> "Here lies the body of D. C. Oaks,
> Who was engaged in that d—d hoax—
> Dead, and in Hell, I suppose."

Neither Mr. Oaks nor Mr. Barker have "crossed the range" yet, but still live to relate scores of good stories of early times, for which we have not the space.

While some were returning disgusted, and others laboring in the lean gravel of Arapahoe and Montana Diggings, others were preparing for more thorough prospecting in the mountains. As early as January, B. F. Langley had found the Deadwood Diggings on South Boulder. Later, George Jackson found the diggings at the mouth of Chicago Creek, on South Clear Creek, near Idaho. But at that season neither could be made to yield much gold. This, briefly, was the situation before the discovery of the

GOLD MINES OF GILPIN COUNTY.

In the latter part of March, a government train passing from Fort Laramie to Fort Union, brought along a man, who had heard of the gold-hunters on the Platte, and who wished to join his fortunes with theirs. He was a Georgian, a returned Californian, who had drifted westward to Fort Leavenworth, had driven a team from Leavenworth to Laramie—some say with a hope of continuing his journey to Frazer river—and now destitute of provisions, and nearly so of clothing, he fell among friends, who needed his help as much as he needed theirs. Although experienced in prospecting, he evinced very little ambition to distinguish himself in that line. This man was

JOHN H. GREGORY.

After lying around the camp at Arapahoe for a month, during which time he was provided for by Captain Sopris and others,

F. KRUSE

GREGORY POINT,

—DEALER IN—

Groceries, Provisions,

TOBACCOS AND CIGARS,

Queen's, Glass, Wooden, Willow and Tinware.

CHOICE TEAS A SPECIALTY.

FRESH BUTTER AND EGGS ALWAYS ON HAND.

it was strongly intimated that he would do well to go out and prospect or "move on." Wilkes Defrees and brother, of South Bend, Indiana, fitted out Gregory and a companion, named William Kendall, for a prospecting trip up Clear Creek. With two white mules, provisions for several days and their prospecting tools, they worked their way through the canyon and on the mountain sides. Doubtless they were the first white men that ever threaded their way through the tortuous defile that excites the admiration and awe of the traveler on the Colorado Central line. Arriving at the forks of the creek, fourteen miles from the entrance to the canyon, the prospect pan invited them up the north fork, or North Clear Creek. Six miles further up, the same guide led them up the gulch which has ever since borne Gregory's name. In the dry gulch opposite the Briggs mill they found such remarkble prospects as to convince them of the existence of a large rich lode near by. After panning out several dollars' worth of gold, and enduring an April snow storm of much severity, they returned to the valley, blazing their way over the hills as they went, and carrying the evidence of their discovery.

Gregory's report of his discovery, although not fully believed, was acted upon. A party was at once formed, consisting of Wilkes Defrees and brother, Dr. Casto, James D. Wood, H. P. A. Smith, C. H. Butler, James Hunter, C. Dean, Captain Bates, Charles Tascher, and perhaps others, which outfitted with two yoke of oxen attached to a pair of forward wheels, and some pack animals. Guided by Gregory, whose trail was chosen on the least wooded ground, they climbed the mountain north of Golden Gate, came into Eight-Mile canyon where the toll-road leaves it, followed up to the head of the gulch and along the ridge a mile, came into Guy gulch, from which they crossed over to Ralston creek, thence up Ralston to Dory hill, taking the hill-side near Sam Haubrich's brewery and crossing over the ridge, reached North Clear Creek at a point near the M. E. Church, Black Hawk. Poor engineering perhaps, but there was no time to chop their way through twenty-five miles of wooded gulches, and so they took the "high line." The journey required four days of severe labor. Captain Sopris went in by way of the Chicago

THROUGH BOULDER CANON.

CARIBOU STAGE COMPANY,

CARRYING U. S. MAILS AND OWN EXPRESS.

Daily to Nederland, Caribou and Boulder.

W. H. & LEON SMITH, Proprietors.

M. SCHULZ,

—DEALER IN—

BOOTS and SHOES,

RUBBER GOODS, ETC.

Mullen Block, — — *CENTRAL CITY.*

FINE GOODS A SPECIALTY.

WM. T. NEWELL,

Manufacturer and Dealer in

All Kinds of Lumber,

MINE AND MILL TIMBERS.

Yards on Eureka street,

CENTRAL CITY, COL.

bar diggings, taking Messrs. Slaughter and Allen, his partners, to the new diggings, arriving soon after the others. The

DISCOVERY OF THE GREGORY LODE

occurred on the 6th of May, 1859, the day following the arrival of the main party. The first panfull from the lode yielded about four dollars. Gregory was greatly excited, and his expressions on seeing the gold all over the bottom of the pan, would be pronounced very profane history indeed, and not altogether delicate. No doubt that he comprehended the value and possibilities of the discovery better than his associates.

In the seventeen years since this discovery, scores of wonderful lodes have been discovered in this and other counties, and while interested parties may, and will deny that this has never had a successful rival, none will deny that, considering the inexperience, isolation and comparative poverty of the pioneers, the Gregory lode was the most available spot to which they could have been directed by the overruling Power. The same may be truthfully said of this county as compared with other counties. California gulch and other tributaries of the Arkansas, Blue, Swan and Snake rivers, furnished extensive and rich diggings, but were far less accessible. What could the pioneers have done with the tellurides of Sunshine and Gold Hill, the silver ores of Georgetown and Caribou, and Park county, or even with the riches of the San Juan country? The large masses of decomposed surface ore, carrying free gold, the rich placer mines, the low altitude of about 8,000 feet above the level of the sea and 2,000 feet above the plain, the short distance of twenty-five miles from the foot of the mountains, and the abundance of timber and water, conspired to make this the most available region yet known. Neither machinery, nor capital, nor experience were essential to success, and as a result, immigration commenced to roll in like a flood.

Returning to details, we find it recorded that the first forty pans of dirt from the Gregory lode, yielded forty dollars. Representatives of larger parties returned to the valley for supplies, and to inform their partners of the welcome facts, and soon the entire movable population was *en route* for

—THE—
Hazard Powder
COMPANY.

THEIR AGENTS:

Solomon Bros., cor. 15th and Larimer sts.,	Denver
W. P. McKinney & Co.,	Boulder
A. F. Curtis,	Georgetown
J. G. Brooks,	Alma
G. S. Barnes,	Colorado Springs
Thatcher Bros.,	Pueblo
Herman Shiffer & Co.,	Del Norte
Hertzinger & Harter,	Caribou

J. O. RAYNOLDS, General Agent, Central City.

This Powder does its own BLOWING and writes its own POETRY.

The best quality of Fuse always on hand at agencies.

W. O. McFarlane.   Peter McFarlane.   A. A. McFarlane.

McFarlane Bros.,

CARPENTERS,   BUILDERS,

CONTRACTORS AND MILLWRIGHTS.

Plans and Specifications furnished for Buildings, Mill and Mine work furnished when desired.

MOULDING, BLINDS and DOORS ALWAYS ON HAND.

Office and Shop on Eureka street, Central City.

Gregory Diggings. Mr. E. W. Henderson, now Receiver in the Land Office at Central, and his party, had the honor of bringing in the first wagon which was ever "snubbed" down the precipitous declivities of the old "Gregory trail." The toll road of later times was not open for travel, until a month or two later, and the character of the first roads may be inferred from the fact that twenty yoke of oxen were required to haul in a small boiler.

The outcrop of the lodes being plain and strong, new discoveries took place in rapid succession. The Bates lode was found on the 15th, the Smith on the 20th, the Dean and the Casto on the 22d, the Gunnell, Kansas, and Burroughs on the 25th, etc., etc. Nearly all of the since notable lodes, and many that have not become famous, were found and opened before the end of June. The Bobtail had a less marked outcrop, and was not discovered till into June, when it was uncovered by a Mr. Cotton. The first pay dirt was hauled down to the gulch for sluicing, with a bobtailed ox in harness, the quartz wagon being a forked stick with a raw hide stretched upon it. This unique outfit suggested to the mind of Captain Parks, the euphonious cognomen of "Bobtail," and the name stuck and was so recorded.

Notwithstanding the facility with which lodes were found, Gregory was in great demand among the inexperienced prospectors, and was often paid two hundred dollars per day for his services.

SLUICING FROM THE GREGORY

commenced on the 16th of May, with five men, and on the 23d they cleaned up $972. Another run of five days, by the same party, yielded $942. Pages of well authenticated statements of yields by sluicing might be given, but it must suffice for comparison with other districts, to state, that before the first of July there were not less than one hundred sluices running in Gregory gulch and below, and that the production was from $20 to $30 per day to the hand. The yield of dirt from the Kansas, Gunnell, Burroughs, Clay County, and many others, including some in Russell district, was quite as large. It is well to note these facts for comparison with the statements from new, remote and altitudinous camps, which are

1876. *1876.*

—THE—
CENTRAL DRUG STORE

Has constantly on hand a full and complete stock of

Pure Drugs and Medicines,

PAINTS, OILS, VARNISHES, QUICKSILVER,

MILL CHEMICALS,

FANCY GOODS, STATIONERY, ETC.

Landreths' Famous Garden and Grass Seeds,

In large or small quantities, which are offered very cheap.

HARVEY M. BURRELL,

CENTRAL CITY.

heralded with all the force that striking head lines with many marks of astonishment can give. We have no disposition to disparage any section of our mining country; neither should it be forgotten that the mines of this county, in all the elements that make mines profitable, have not been equalled by any other discoveries in Colorado.

THE FIRST ORGANIZATION

of Gregory District took place on the 16th of May, when there were but sixteen men in the camp. Wilkes Defrees was chosen President of the district. No records are extant, but it is known that the number and size of lode, gulch, and building claims were then agreed upon, as they were afterward established by popular vote. By June 1st, the camp had increased to 800 or 1,000 men. The late arrivals set up a clamor that the first-comers had "gobbled up" all the good lodes. They demanded a redistribution of lode property, giving each one twenty-five linear feet on the vein. About the 15th of June, a mass meeting was held to determine the question. By this time the malcontents outnumbered those interested in maintaining one hundred feet as the length of a lode claim, as ten to one. Among the early pioneers, however, were many old political wire-workers, men accustomed to lead mass meetings and manipulate conventions. This handful of men succeeded in obtaining control of the meeting, by the election of Wilkes Defrees, chairman, and James D. Wood, secretary. The "twenty-five-foot" men demanded that the lodes should be re-staked by those who could reach them first, and in anticipation of an easy victory, members of every party or firm in their number, went out in advance with an axe and stakes in hand, ready to drive them upon the best ground, the moment they got the signal from their friends that the measure was carried! But the race was not to the swift. The adroit and cool-headed pioneers succeeded in carrying a vote to have a committee of twelve on resolutions appointed, and a majority of their own number were assigned to that committee. Casto, Gregory, Slaughter, Allen, Sopris, Barker, Bates, Henderson, Russell, and three others were the committee chosen. Of course, this committee reported resolutions confirming all the rights they had previously claimed.

J. COLLIER,
PHOTOGRAPHER,
Main Street, Central City.

Publisher of Rocky Mountain Scenery.

N. A. SEARS,
Contractor & Builder,
CENTRAL CITY, COLORADO.

Plans and Specifications furnished when desired.

WM. WOODRUFF,
HOUSE AND SIGN PAINTER,
Paper-Hanger and Calciminer.

Shop opposite the National Hotel, Central City.

S. P. KENDALL,
WATCHMAKER.
OPPOSITE CITY BOOK STORE,

Main Street, - - - Central City.

A. BITZENHOFER'S
WESTERN BAKERY,
Dostal Block, Main Street, Central City.

Wheat, Rye and Graham Bread constantly on hand. Also, Pies and Cakes.

The discussion that ensued was, to speak mildly, a spirited one. Before the vote on each resolution was taken, the managers took pains to raise side issues, getting their opponents separated and squabbling among themselves, when the resolution would be pronounced "carried," with great force and dignity. Outgeneraled and angry, the crowd was a turbulent one. Every man had his six-shooter with him in those days, and no less pluck and determination were shown in maintaining the action of the meeting, than there had been of cunning and adroitness in securing the result. But the occasion passed without a fight, and soon the malcontents became owners of claims of their own finding, and were no longer Agrarians. The segregation of lodes into claims of one hundred feet, has since been found a great mistake, and the law has been changed; but those who bemoan the early division as disastrous to prosperity, will see that it was the best that could be done.

On the 9th of July, another mass meeting was held, at which were elected by ballot, a president, Captain Richard Sopris, a recorder of claims, Dr. C. A. Roberts, and a sheriff, Charles Peck, to serve one year. A committee was appointed to codify the laws, which had now obtained general consent, and were adopted without opposition. This code formed the model of the laws of the several districts which during the fall were set off from Gregory District, viz: Eureka, Nevada, Central City, Lake and Quartz Valley. These "local laws" were subsequently confirmed by the first Territorial Legislature, and were recognized by Congressional enactment when not in conflict with existing statutes.

Early in the fall of 1859, several arastras were put in operation below Black Hawk, working the headings from the sluices and the quartz from the lodes. These were quite successful in saving the gold, but their speed is only suited to the Mexican, to whom a day is as a thousand years and *vice versa*. Some unique contrivances for quartz crushing might have been seen in those days. One Mr. Red exhibited the quality of his genius in a trip-hammer, pivoted on a stump, the hammer-head pounding quartz in a wooden trough. For obvious reasons this was dubbed the "Woodpecker mill." The

ROLLINS HOUSE,

—AT—

ROLLINSVILLE, GILPIN COUNTY.

This is a first-class country hotel, situated in a beautiful mountain valley on South Boulder Creek, twelve miles from Central and Black Hawk, at the junction of the Rollinsville and Middle Park Wagon Road with the Caribou road. Its attractions are fine scenery, pure air, clear water, green meadows, fair trout fishing and hunting, clean, airy rooms, and a good table. Accessible by daily line of stages (bringing daily mail) from Black Hawk, Central and Boulder; also, by stage line from Middle Park.

JOHN Q. A. ROLLINS, Proprietor.

Z. MYERS,

Dealer in and Manufacturer of

BOOTS and SHOES

LEATHER FINDINGS,

RUBBER GOODS.

FINE GOODS A SPECIALTY.

Gregory Street,   *BLACK HAWK.*

FIRST QUARTZ MILL

was a home-made six-stamper, built by Charles Giles, of Galway county, Ohio, run by water power, and situated near the mouth of Chase gulch. The stamp-stems—shod with iron—the cam-shaft, cams, and mortar were of wood. This rude concern netted the owner $6,000 that summer and fall.

The first imported mill was the little three-stamper of T. T. Prosser, which was set up in Prosser gulch, about the middle of September. Coleman & Le Fevre brought in a six-stamp mill, which was first set up just above the present Briggs mill, and afterwards removed to and run with the Prosser mill. In November, this mill was producing from Gunnell quartz from $60 to $100 per ton, the gold being saved in riffles supplied with quicksilver. It would be interesting to know what such quartz would yield in a modern mill. Next, Mr. Ridgeway got his six-stamp wooden mill into operation on Clear Creek, below Black Hawk. Then about the 6th of December, came the Clark, Vandeventer & Co. nine-stamp mill, built by Gates & Co., of Chicago, the first regular foundry-built mill in the country. This was set up at the junction of Eureka and Spring gulches, in the heart of the present city of Central. The success of these first mills was sufficient to convince every man that all he needed to acquire a fortune, was a quartz mill. Some notice of the

PLACER MINES

closes the record of 1859. Green Russell, who made the discovery of the Montana Diggings above Denver in 1858, came in from the States about June 1st, 1859, with 170 followers. His party camped in Central, where the Welch row now stands, and one fine morning they "folded their tents like the Arabs and as silently stole away" over to Russell gulch, where they had found rich diggings in the main gulch and its tributaries. By the end of September there were 900 men in that district, and all found profitable work. Here parties produced as high as $35 per day to the hand. Five dollars per day was considered a fair average. This would indicate about $50,000 per week as the maximum production. At the same time, over 200 men were gulch mining on the upper tributaries of Gregory with equal results. The yield of the

WM. SECHRIST,
Merchant Tailor

DENVER, COLORADO.

Will visit Gilpin County. All orders entrusted to his care will be promptly attended to and guaranteed as represented.

Orders taken for Custom Made Shirts at lowest cash prices.

Laflin & Rand Powder Co.,

26 MURRAY STREET, N. Y.

FRESH MINING and BLASTING POWDER

A full assortment of their celebrated Sporting Powder, Electric Batteries and Fuses.

T. D. SEARS, General Agent, Central City.   P. O. Box 348.

United States Mineral and Agricultural Land Agency.

WM. A. ARNOLD,

CENTRAL CITY,   -   *COLORADO.*

Will prepare Mining Applications for Patent, draw up Adverse Claims, make out all papers pertaining to the Pre-emption or Homestead acts, make copies of papers on file in the Land Office, and do a general business as attorney before the United States Land Offices of Colorado.

Office in Schoenecker & Mack's building. Entrance on Pine street.

one hundred claims in Gregory gulch, the four mills and half-dozen arastras, cannot be guessed at so closely as the placer production. There are no means of determining the yield of the mines in those eight months of 1859, as nearly all the gold was taken to the States by private hands. No old settler will estimate the production at less than $500,000, and some claim that $1,000,000 is nearer the proper estimate. We know that John Gregory captured $39,000, and Green Russell about $25,000. Scores left in the autumn with dust enough to purchase and freight out a quartz mill, and nearly every one made a "good stake."

The necessity of a larger supply of water than the gulches afforded, was apparent the first summer. In July, three companies were organized for building ditches, and three ditches were commenced, viz: the Metropolitan, the Russell and the Nevada. The latter was built from North Clear Creek to Nevada, and used until 1861, when after long difficulties with the Black Hawk mill-owners, the use of the ditch was permanently stopped. The two former were consolidated and became the

CONSOLIDATED DITCH,

which is said to have cost $100,000 in labor, but which did not cost the owners half that sum, as so much labor and material were donated. After selling water ever since for $1.00 per inch per 12 hours, the ditch is now for sale to the county for $50,000. The county commissioners have offered $25,000, and rightly stand firm upon their offer.

"SIXTY."

The outlook of this year was full of promise. Mining had been progressing to some extent during the winter, well constructed quartz mills were coming in almost daily, and the Consolidated ditch, now about finished, would supply the gulch miners with all the water needed. By the first of July, sixty mills had been brought into the county, and the immense influx of immigrants made labor cheap and supplies reasonable. The mill men were unacquainted with the use of amalgamated copper-plates for gold-saving. There began to be general complaint that the mills would not save the gold.

WILLIAM RICHARDS,
Plasterer and Calciminer,
Central City, Colorado.

Orders left at Central Drug Store will receive prompt attention.

D. S. McKENNEY'S
LIVERY AND FEED STABLE
GREGORY STREET, CENTRAL.

Stylish Turn-outs furnished on reasonable terms.

ICE! ICE! ICE!

Ice furnished families, hotels, and saloons on short notice.

Leave orders at Hawley & Manville's, Central, and Hughes' "Little Market," Black Hawk.

N. A. SEARS.

WILSON BROS.,
DAIRYMEN,
CENTRAL CITY, - COLORADO.

Fresh pure Milk furnished families, hotels and restaurants.

Will also deliver clear and soft spring water.

F. PFLUM,
Manufacturer and Dealer in
BOOTS AND SHOES
RUBBER GOODS AND LEATHER FINDINGS.

Miners' wear a specialty.   Lawrence street, CENTRAL.

Pyrites of iron and copper were reached in many of the older lodes, and because little or no gold could be saved in the riffles from the "iron," as it was called, it was believed to be not only worthless, but a material foreign to the vein matter, that had somehow displaced for a time the gold-bearing quartz. A subscription was made and work actually commenced on the Gregory, to sink through the pyrites to the brown quartz! Nothing better illustrates the universal ignorance of the whole business at that time, than the facts above stated. Generally, when the sulphurets were reached, work was suspended. Still, 1860 was a prosperous year. There was still a plenty of surface quartz, and the gulches being more systematically worked, with an abundant supply of water, yielded a very large return. It was the great year of immigration. Men and families came in, built houses, shops and stores, until the entire length of all the gulches was "settled" upon. Thousands came that found no work, and poured out into new camps, or to find new mines in unprospected districts.

Notwithstanding the general backset before the close of the year, on account of the failure of the mills to save gold from the pyritous ore, the remarkable sluice yields of the previous year were supplemented with no less remarkable mill runs from the same and other lodes. On Burroughs quartz, an eight-hours run with six stamps, produced $321.55; a twelve-hours run produced $400, and one hundred and fifty tons of the same produced $4,400. Fiske lode quartz yielded $20 per ton, which may perhaps be taken as an average, the range being from $7 to $90 per ton. This, it should be remembered, was realized before the introduction of amalgamated copperplates, or of uniformly fine screens. Will some San Juan enthusiast try a few tons of Little Annie quartz, in such a mill, by way of comparison?

The most noteworthy event in the milling business of 1861, was the use of amalgamated sheet copper for gold-saving. Like many other things well understood in mining countries, the pioneers then first learned its value. So immediately apparent was the advantage in its use, that copper sold from four to seven dollars per pound for this purpose. But a fair success was by no means immediate. No one knew the business,

WARNER & SCOBEY,

Importers and Wholesale and Retail Dealers in

Wines, Liquors,

CIGARS AND TOBACCO,

AT THE VERY LOWEST PRICES.

Four doors below their old stand,

Gregory Street, - **BLACK HAWK.**

☞ *The only wholesale house in Black Hawk.* ☜

H. J. KRUSE & CO.,

Wholesale and Retail Dealers in

Staple and Fancy Groceries,

CROCKERY, GLASSWARE,

TOBACCO, CIGARS, WOOD AND WILLOW WARE,

CONFECTIONERY, ETC.

Agents for Dupont's Powder.

GREGORY ST., (*foot bridge from Lawrence st.,*) CENTRAL.

and the measure of success subsequently attained, was the result of patient and persevering experimenting, which cost in lost treasure more than was saved. There are no statistics of yields extant from which the average of these years can be calculated. We have it recorded, however, that one hundred and eighty tons of Gold Dirt ore yielded $34 per ton; twenty tons of Bobtail ore, $94 per ton; five tons of same, $260 per ton, and one ton selected and run upon a wager, over $600 per ton. The average yield, however, was probably below $15 per ton. Only a few mills were doing good work even for that time, and many were so badly constructed that good work was impossible.

Then came another backset. The deeper mines "went into cap." This term was applied indiscriminately to cases where the vein matter became too lean for profitable working, and where the vein became "pinched" below a profitable working width. Hundreds gave up all effort against such a sea of difficulties, and scattered out to avail themselves of surface workings in newer fields. Other hundreds attempted to "sink through cap" with too short a purse, and failed. Some who had husbanded their profits, were able to continue until their veins "opened out" or "struck pay" again.

The gulch mines were not yet exhausted, and with the improved methods, were much more prosperous as a rule than lode mines.

The year 1862 brought a more hopeful feeling among the lode miners. Several prominent mines passed through the cap, and were now producing better than ever. The mines were from 100 to 200 feet deep, and no one questioned their permanence. Probably twenty mines could be selected, the ores from which yielded from $20 to $30 per ton; the others from $10 to $20. The premium on gold rising more rapidly than prices of labor and supplies, further stimulated activity. The mill process was now generally understood, and the gulch mines still gave employment to hundreds of men.

On the other hand, there were ores shown to be rich by assay, from which the stamp process would extract but little gold. The increasing depths of the mines made steam power

CALIFORNIA POWDER WORKS

—AND—

California Fuse Works.

THEIR AGENTS FOR SELLING

Hercules, Blasting, Sporting Powder and Fuse.

I. Brinker & Co., 367 and 369 Larimer St.,	Denver
F. A. Squires,	Boulder
M. C. Kirby,	Golden
Chas. R. Fish,	Georgetown
Harris & Moynahan,	Alma
Peyton & Hanawalt,	Saguache
T. O'Connell	Del Norte

Being the best Powder and Fuse that comes into the Territory.

WM. LARNED, General Agent, Central City.

MACHINE POETRY NO. 77.

Hercules! sing me a song,
   Thrilling with power's delight—
For you have dawned on the miner's morn,
   And given him a powder right.
The fiddle allures in vain,
   And not silent is the liar,
But blow drill holes out again,
   Which charms the miner's desire;
You shatter the rock, and I fear
   The storm of rolling ore,
While I watch Hercules Powder, my dear,
   I'm happy for evermore.

indispensable. The water was increasing. Unskillful timbering must be renewed, and shafts must be straightened for permanent work. These things did not diminish faith in mining, but began to be talked of as evidence that "poor men have no business to pursue mining."

The year 1863 was a fairly prosperous one. Lode mining was on the increase, and gulch mining profitable, though of limited amount. Gold still advanced more rapidly than prices of supplies, reaching 172, and averaging 145 through the year. Late in the summer and fall, a few mines were sold to companies in New York and Boston, the first being the Ophir mine on the Burroughs. The

STOCK MANIA OF "SIXTY-FOUR"

then commenced, and raged until some time in April, when the "bottom fell out of everything." During this time nearly all the developed mining property in the county, and a much larger amount of wholly undeveloped claims, changed hands. Valuable improved property sold as high as $1,000 per linear foot, and "wild-cat" claims—bonded by the score without reference to contiguity—sold ten thousand times higher in proportion to their value. It appeared that the Eastern promoters wanted anything upon which stock might be issued; the people wanted anything in exchange for the rapidly depreciating greenbacks; and the mine-owners—well, they were not afraid of greenbacks, providing the pile was large enough.

One example—not an exceptional one—will illustrate the sale and stocking of mines in 1864. A mining firm which had taken $50,000 from their property, but had exhausted their profit in sinking through a "pinch," bonded their property for $40,000. It consisted of four thousand feet on fifteen different lodes, only one of which was developed. Being late in the market, the Colorado operator was very glad to close out to a pool for $50,000. Stocked at $500,000, four-fifths of the shares were sold for $200,000. Subsequently, two companies with a capital stock of $500,000 each, were organized upon detached and undeveloped portions of the property, and from the sale of shares in these, some

Chas. Johnson,

Wholesale and Retail Dealer in

BOOTS AND SHOES,

Rubber Goods, Etc.

No. 400 Lawrence Street,

(Next door to DANIELS, FISHER & CO.,)

DENVER. - COLORADO.

Henry Crow, Prest.   J. S. Brown, Vice Prest.
John R. Hanna, Cashier.   S. A. Herrick, Ass't Cashier.

—THE—

CITY NATIONAL BANK

DENVER, COLORADO.

DIRECTORS:

Henry Grow.   J. S. Brown.   E. A. Newton.
Jno. R. Hanna.   Wm. Barth.

New York Correspondent--NATIONAL PARK BANK.

$37,500 more were realized. It is hoped it will not be impertinent to ask, Who were the "swindlers" of the "widows and orphans" in this case? Colorado operators cannot claim the credit of getting up this wild excitement. On arriving in New York, they found themselves powerless without the aid of some experienced broker, who operated with a pool, each member of which was the bell-wether of a flock of investors; and both must have failed, but for the flood of depreciated and still depreciating currency, seeking investment.

It should not be understood that all the investments made in our mines were for purely speculative purposes. Some bought good property at fair rates as an investment; really intended to work their mines for a profit; put up working capital; employed honest, capable, and as far as was possible, experienced agents. Why, then, it may be asked, did these working companies fail of dividends? From the standpoint of the present, it is difficult to understand why any other result could have been looked for.

The first cause of failure was the war and its consequences. Prices of labor and supplies of all kinds had by that time reached a price corresponding with the highest price of gold, and owing to the distance from the base of supplies did not fluctuate and fall with gold. Laborers in all departments were in great demand, on account of the immense amount of new work commencing, and readily commanded as an average price $5.00 per day, while their desire to earn their wages was in the inverse ratio. The prices of supplies were enormous. Mules and horses sold for $400@$500, each; wood, $12 per cord; hay, $120@$250 per ton; corn, 12@20 cents per lb.; flour, $25@$30 per 100 lbs.; candles, $16@$30 per box of 40 lbs.; steel, 60@75 cents per lb.; powder, $12@$15 per keg; fuse, $4.00 per hundred feet; iron, 30@35 cents per lb.; lumber, $60 per M, and all other supplies in proportion. It should be observed, that the high prices of 1864-'6 were not wholly chargeable to the war, but were enhanced by the difficulties of wagon transportation through six hundred miles of hostile Indian country, the main road through which was in the sole possession of the Indians for two months in 1864.

TELLER HOUSE

BARBER AND BATH ROOMS,

JONES & URICK, - PROPRIETORS,

Hot and Cold Shower Baths. Basement of Teller House.

B. F. PEASE,

Dry Goods, Yankee Notions, Boots and Shoes

LADIES' AND GENT'S FURNISHING GOODS.

McFarlane Block, Main Street, CENTRAL CITY.

W. C. HENDRICKS,
Agent for

The Singer Sewing Machines, Chickering Pianos, Estey, Burdett, Mason & Hamlin Organs.

Office at Central Drug Store, Central City.

"THE BELVIDERE."

An elegantly furnished Hall and Stage, seating about 400 persons, well-ventilated and lighted, and contains a new grand piano-forte.

Lock Box 394. **H. M. TELLER & S. B. HAHN, Proprs.**

MOUNTAIN CITY CASH STORE,

C. C. MILLER, - **PROPRIETOR,**

Groceries, Provisions, Canned and Dried Fruits, Glass, Nails, Tobacco, Cigars, Furnishing Goods.

CENTRAL CITY, COL.

Another cause of failure, was the absence of smelting works or any other reduction works, for the suitable treatment of the richest portion of the ore. This brought upon us a horde of

PROCESS MEN.

Indeed, the plague began in 1863, and lasted as long as there was money to be wasted. Pans of every name and pattern were in use in the mills, were piled around them and garnished the wayside. Keith desulphurizers loomed up here and there; Crosby & Thompson roasting cylinders, thirty sets in all, infested every district; Bertola's miniature pans and process delighted ladies and children; and the Monnier—but why finish the list? Were they not all devourers of greenbacks, giving little or no gold in return?

If, then, war prices, a distant purchase market, Indian war, processes, hard winters, wet summers, ignorance of the business, and last, though not least, "conducting the war from Vienna," were sufficient to break the well-organized, solid companies, what could be expected of the "kiting" class? What could be expected of a company which paid $60,000 for sixty wild-cat claims on as many different lodes? Or what of that numerous class of company's agents, the "jolly dogs"— usually nephew of the president, or son of the head director— excellent masters of the billiard cue, with uncommon pride in high boots and spurs, whose champagne bills were charged to "candles," and whose costly incense to Venus appeared on the books as "cash paid for mercury"? It was a charming farce to witness a General Fitz John and staff of assistants, all finely mounted, reviewing the corps of masons on the stone "folly," or riding to and from the mine; but was it business? And those spectacled "professors," with their heads in the clouds and the most honest intentions in their hearts: what good did their costly experiments ever do, but to show "how not to do it"? But whether agents worked faithfully or played at doing business, all roads seemed to end in comparative failure, if not disaster. Company after company retired from the field disgusted, until at one time, five or six years after the stock mania, but one foreign mining corporation was doing business in Gilpin county. That, the Bobtail Gold

Mosley & Ballard,

BLACK HAWK, COL.,

CONTRACTORS and BUILDERS

―――DEALERS IN ALL KINDS OF―――

LUMBER,

Sash, Doors and Blinds.

Office on Clear Creek adjoining Boiler Works.

Mining Company, Mr. A. N. Rogers, Manager, never suspended, and is to-day one of the most prosperous concerns in the county.

The capital stock of the mining companies in this county aggregated abont $100,000,000. A large number of the companies never made a move towards business. Another large percentage did business with great spirit, chiefly in the mill building line, till the managers unloaded their shares. The percentage that tried honestly and in a business-like way, to make a success, was small.

LYON'S SMELTING WORKS,

upon which the hopes of the people were wrecked, were built in 1865, and continued in a state of intermittent operation and change till the end of 1866, when they were closed permanently, and the property passed into the hands of the Consolidated Gregory Company. From all these failures we gladly turn to what has been properly called a

GENERAL REVIVAL

of the mining business, which had its beginning in 1868. There were hundreds of miners and workmen of all kinds, and scores of agents, thrown upon their own resources. The mines were considerably opened and provided with machinery. The mills were idle. Every one saw that it was a country of great possibilities, and realized the effect of completed railroads and successful smelting works. All had learned something from the failures of the past. As the work of companies on their own account gradually ceased, the system of

LEASING MINES

came in vogue. The agents or owners leased the mines or parts of them to the miners, principally Cornishmen, for a percentage of the proceeds. Properties that had steadily absorbed the product or more, now began to yield a small revenue to the owners. It was soon discovered, however, that the short leases worked a damage to the mines. There was no incentive to open new ground, to do permanent timbering or even to conserve the property. Gradually from that time to the present, one mine after another has been reopened under leases, running from one to five years, all the time

F. J. BARTLE,

—DEALER IN—

Groceries, Provisions, Liquors

Cigars, Tobacco, Glass and Queensware.

A large assortment of Native and Foreign Ftuits in cans and glass, and Family Supplies of all kinds always kept on hand.

THE LARGEST HOUSE IN NEVADA, COL.

SHANSTROM BROS.,

—DEALERS IN—

Meats, Poultry, Fish

AND VEGETABLES.

CENTRAL CITY and MAIN STREET, NEVADA.

R. E. WHITSITT,

—DEALER IN—

Denver City Real Estate,

RIETHMANN BLOCK,

Corner Fifteenth and Arapahoe Streets,

DENVER, - COLORADO.

tending to longer leases. Many of the superintendents and owners who at first lacked the necessary experience, are now very successful lessees and are working on a large scale. It is believed that one-half or more of the present bullion product of the county is from the work of lessees.

CONSOLIDATION

of adjoining properties upon the same lode has been another fruitful source of the increased and increasing prosperity of the business. The Bobtail Gold Mining Company, which at first owned but 433½ feet, have absorbed by consolidation and purchase, other properties on the same lode, till now they own 900 feet. The Briggs Brothers, by purchase of the Black Hawk Gregory and lease of the Consolidated Gregory, now control and work 1,040 feet of that great lode and 400 feet of a smaller vein. The Buell mine, consisting of 3,000 linear feet of lode property adjoining and contiguous, is an example of consolidation by purchase. Six hundred feet of the Burroughs lode, belonging to two different companies, are under a thirty-two-years' lease to Sullivan & Co., a good example of consolidation by leasing. The relocation of abandoned property under the act of Congress of 1872 and Territorial legislation in conformity thereto, has resulted in numerous consolidations of detached claims. Several such properties are now producing liberally. The completion of two

RAILROADS

to Denver in 1870, and the building of the Colorado Central railroad into the county in 1873, were indispensable to the success of mining. The reduction in wages, in the prices of mine and mill supplies, and in the cost of living, due directly to the cheaper transportation, will be seen by an examination of the following table, comparing the prices in 1866, (the last year of freighting by wagon the whole distance from the Missouri river,) with prices at the present time. In 1866 gold was about 140, and this year say 113. Therefore, about 20 per cent. of the reduction is chargeable to the difference in gold, and the balance to the difference in cost of transportation.

Jas. M. Bible.   S. C. Huntington.   J. L. Taylor.

JAS. M. BIBLE & CO.,

Black Hawk Foundry,

Manufacturers of Milling and Mining Machinery.

BLACK HAWK,   -   *COLORADO.*

JOHN TOMLINSON,

GENERAL BLACKSMITH.

ALL KINDS OF HEAVY FORGING.

Mining Tools &c. Made to Order.

SHOP AT BIBLE & CO'S FOUNDRY.

BLACK HAWK,   -   *COLORADO.*

GEORGE STROEHLE,

—MANUFACTURER OF—

Boilers and Smoke-stacks

REPAIRING DONE ON SHORT NOTICE.

Works foot of Gregory St.,   *BLACK HAWK.*

Articles.	1866.	1876.
Labor per day	$4@$5	$2.50@$3
Lumber, per M	$60	$20
Flour, per sack	$20@$24	$4.25@$5
Corn, per ℔	13@18c	1¾@2
Hay, per ton	$80@$100	$30
Candles, per box	$18@$20	$7.50
Powder, per keg	$10@$12	$4.25
Fuse, per 1,000 feet	$30@$40	$9@$12
Sheet Copper, per ℔	80c@$1.00	36c@40c
Nails, " "	20c@25c	5¼c
Iron, " "	25c@30c	7½c
Sheet iron, " "	35c	5¼c
Quicksilver, " "	$1.65@$2.00	90c
Wood, per cord	$8	$5.50
Coal oil, per gal	$2.75@$3.00	33@35c
Lard, " "	" "	$1.30@$1.50
Shovels	$2.75	$1.25@$1.75
Picks	$3.50@$3.75	$1.50
Bellows, 36-inch	$50	$25
Anvils, per ℔	40c	19c
Rope, " "	60c	18c

The next, and one of the most important factors in a calculation of the causes which have produced the changes of the last ten years, is the establishment of a home market for our richest and most refractory ores. The value of

THE BOSTON AND COLORADO SMELTING WORKS

to this county, and several others, can hardly be overstated. The

SAMPLING WORKS

of Mr. Bertolin at Black Hawk, furnish a market for about two hundred tons per month, principally galenous ore. This ore is forwarded to the Golden Smelting Works, managed by Messrs. Young and West. Another very noticeable cause of the increased success of late years, is found in the improvements made in

STAMP MILLS,

and the mode of working. It will not be considered an exaggeration to say, that the present average yield from the same ore

WILLIAM AITCHESON,

Manufacturing

JEWELER AND WATCHMAKER,

CENTRAL CITY, COLORADO.

Dealer in Watches, Clocks, Spectacles, Silver Ware, Cutlery Fishing Tackle, Etc. Native Gold Jewelry made. Notary Seals cut.

SWANSEA SMELTING WORKS

DENVER, - COLORADO.

BUYS ORES CONTAINING GOLD, SILVER, COPPER AND LEAD.

W. Lawson, Proprietor.   S. Balbach, Superintendent.

NEUMANN & FOLSTER,

Proprietors of

UNION BAKERY,

Cracker Manufacturers and Grocers.

Lawrence Street,   CENTRAL CITY.

C. F. BURRELL,

IMPORTING TAILOR,

389 LAWRENCE STREET,

DENVER - - COLORADO.

T. S. CLAYTON,

"THE HATTER,"

264 Fifteenth St., 1st store above Larimer,

DENVER, - - COLORADO.

is 25 per cent. better than the yield of ten years ago. The

COLLOM CONCENTRATING WORKS

at Black Hawk, for the treatment of low grade ores, are attracting much attention. These works, with the smelting works and mills, form the subjects of separate chapters, and therefore details are omitted here.

During the past ten years some foreign capital has been invested in the smelting and concentration business, but scarcely any in the purchase and working of mines. All parts of the business have been studied with a dilligence born of necessity, and with a growing conviction now amounting to certainty that legitimate mining *will pay.* Owing to the fact that the reduction of ores and mining are now generally independent pursuits, the necessity for a large capital no longer exists. Still, a moderate capital is necessary, otherwise it would not long remain true that not over 10 per cent. of the well-known good mines are in operation. The time has been that a piece of mining property—no matter if it had been productive ground once—had no marketable value. But this state of things is now changing, and the change in the future will be more rapid. No one expects or wishes the excitement of 1864 to return, but as gold mining in this county has recovered in a manner from the disasters of the speculative period, and can look the world in the face again, the attention and closest scrutiny of business men with capital are again invited to the mines of Gilpin county.

Hermann H. Heiser,

―MANUFACTURER OF―

CALIFORNIA SADDLES

AND HARNESS OF EVERY DESCRIPTION.

FINE HARNESS A SPECIALTY.

Wholesale and Retail Dealer in

Whips, Lashes, Saddlery Hardware and Horse Clothing.

AGENT J. R. HILL & CO'S "CONCORD HARNESS."

378 Blake St.,   **DENVER, COL.**

LODES.

To give even a condensed history of all the well-known and prominent lodes in the county, would require at least a year's time and two hundred such pages as this. An exhaustive history of any one great lode would require more space, than in the design of this book, has been allotted to the chapter. The only course possible is to select such representative lodes—not all the largest and most productive either in the present or past—as will show samples, as it were, of various classes. Scores of valuable lodes might be named, but with no data of production or yield per ton, no desirable information is given. To have one's inquiries answered by guesses at dates and dimensions, and estimates from memory of production and yield, is far from satisfactory. Again, to give the entire and exact production of any lode is impossible, as the facts are not attainable; but where the full production is estimated, the result is as exact as it can be made. With this understanding with the reader, we proceed to notice more particularly a *very few* lodes, conscious that such condensed and imcomplete statements do no sort of justice to the properties, and well aware that the list of unmentioned lodes embraces scores of the first rank.

To avoid repetition, it may be remarked here that the general characteristics of all the lodes are the same. The country rock, chiefly granite, with some gneissic varieties: course, east and west, or from 10° to 15° north of east and south of west: dip, nearly vertical, rarely reaching an angle of 15°, possessing all the characteristics of true fissure veins, and notably free from faults.

The productive portion of the veins commonly carries a vein of solid pyrites, enclosed in or upon the side of the quartzose and feldspathic mixture, having pyrites more or less

M. F. BEBEE,
—DEALER IN—

Horses, Wagons and Mules

STABLE ON GREGORY ST., BLACK HAWK.

Also, does Quartz Hauling and Express business. Will contract for Mine and Mill Timbers.

☞ Tourists furnished with Turn-outs on short notice.

CHANDLER FREEMAN,
—DEALER IN—

Books and Stationery,

TOYS, CUTLERY, FANCY GOODS,

Mountain Views, Wall Paper, Picture Frames, Etc.

Main Street,   CENTRAL CITY.

GEORGE BRUBAKER,
—DEALER IN—

Groceries, Provisions,

QUEENSWARE AND RANCH PRODUCE.

Marsh & Buffington Block,

Gregory Street,   BLACK HAWK.

disseminated through it. The distribution of ore, both horizontally and vertically, is not uniform, sometimes pinching to a mere seam and again opening to twenty feet. The existence of pay chutes or courses of ore, sometimes nearly vertical, in some localities dipping east and in others west, is denied by those only who have failed to make careful observations.

All of the gold-bearing ores contain more or less silver. The percentage of silver in the smelting ores, as compared with the total of gold and silver, is indicated by the following:

In 688 tons of Bobtail ore, of the total assay value in gold and silver, 6 per cent. was silver; in 428 tons of Burroughs ore, 9½ per cent.; in 424 tons of California ore, 28 per cent., and in 95 tons Prize ore, 44 per cent. From the statement of the Boston & Colorado Smelting Company, it appears that of the assay value of the Gilpin county ores purchased, 20 per cent. was silver; but this, doubtless, includes some lots of strictly silver ore.

Mr. George H. Gray, Territorial assayer, in his last annual report, gives the gold and silver values of the mill bullion for 1875, from which it appears that the silver in the mill bullion is about 1½ per cent. Assuming that the mill ore has the same proportion of silver as the smelting ore, and such data as we have proves this to be correct, it is plain that but a small percentage of the silver is amalgamated, and so far throws doubt upon the theory that the silver in the gold-bearing lodes is in the form of an alloy, or free native silver; otherwise, the percentage of silver amalgamated would equal the percentage of gold. The practical conclusion of this is, that ores carrying from 28 to 44 per cent. of the assay value in silver are not adapted to stamp-mill process, but should be treated by concentration.

GREGORY LODE.

Something of the early history of the Gregory may be found in the historical chapter at the commencement of this volume. In 1864, nine mining companies were organized with properties on the Grégory and its extensions for a basis,

H. M. ORAHOOD,

ATTORNEY AT LAW,

CENTRAL CITY, COLORADO.

CHARLES W. HAVENS,

Dealer in

GROCERIES, QUEENSWARE,

HAY AND GRAIN.

Main Street,   *BLACK HAWK.*

WM. McLAUGHLIN,

Manufacturer and Dealer in

Harness, Saddles and Findings,

Lawrence St., Central and Gregory St., Black Hawk.

ED. A. SEIWELL,

Dealer in

DRUGS, PAINTS, OILS, VARNISHES, AND PATENT MEDICINES OF ALL KINDS.

Prescriptions carefully compounded at all hours of the day or night.

GREGORY ST., BLACK HAWK.

IHRIG & SEYMOUR,

Successors to A. G. RHOADS,

Manufacturers of the Celebrated

BLACK HAWK CRACKERS, AND DEALERS IN CRACKERS, BREAD, PIES, CAKES, GROCERIES AND PROVISIONS.

Black Hawk, Colorado.

in all covering about 4,000 linear feet. The principal productive work done, however, has been done upon a little less than a half mile of the vein.

The Black Hawk Company, formerly owning Nos. 1, 2, 3, 16 and 17 west, sold in September, 1874, the first three claims worked to the depth of 600 feet, and equipped with a 14-inch Cornish pump, to the Briggs Bros., who before owned three claims adjoining on the east. The Briggs Bros. also leased the Consolidated Gregory mine, comprising claims 4, 5, 6, 7 and 8 west, thus giving them the ownership of 540 feet, and the management of 1,040 feet. The Smith & Parmelee Company and the New York Company were consolidated some seven or eight years ago, bringing 800 feet under the management of B. T. Wells, Esq., who has proved a successful superintendent. The Narragansett Company's property has been operated more or less under leases of late, thus bringing all of the lode under three managements.

At the present time the main shaft on the New York & Colorado Company's property is 625 feet deep. The workings are drained by a 6-inch Cornish pump. The mine easily supplies mill ore for the 40-stamp mill situated over the mine. The hoisting works, pump and mill are driven by one engine. From thirty to forty tons of ore per day are broken, from which was realized in 1875, the gross amount of $67,310.65, with a large reserve of ore unbroken.

The Briggs Bros. shaft is about 725 feet deep, and levels are to be run westward through the property managed by them. Their production keeps 50 stamps employed, and about $35,000 are annually received for smelting ore. Their total production last year was $134,634.10. The total production of the Gregory for 1875 foots up a trifle more than $225,000, and for 1874 very nearly the same. The present workings of the lode are in large masses of rather low grade ore, the vein in some instances reaching a width of twenty feet.

The total production of the Gregory lode has been from $4,500,000 to $5,000,000. This estimate is made in part by the known production of some years, and in part by comparison of the known with the unknown.

J. D. PEREGRINE,

Civil and Mining Engineer

---AND---

DEPUTY U. S. MINERAL LAND SURVEYOR,

CENTRAL CITY, COLORADO.

---o---

Office, Room No. 10, Harris Block. Entrance on Pine Street. P. O. Box 59.

Black Hawk House,

J. F. Taber, Prop.

THE ONLY FIRST-CLASS HOUSE IN THE CITY.

Livery Stable connected with the House.

EXCURSION PARTIES CAN BE ACCOMMODATED BY TELEGRAPHING.

EVERYTHING FIRST-CLASS

BOBTAIL LODE.

From its discovery in 1859 to 1864, this lode was worked in the irregular manner of that period. The vein was not so large as the Gregory vein, but the quartz was rich and well distributed, so that the production was large. In sluicing the surface dirt, from $20 to $25 per day to the hand was realized for several months. In 1861, Messrs. Lee, Judd & Lee obtained $260 per ton from five tons of selected ore. E. J. Sweet selected twenty cubic feet of copper pyrites from Field's claim that yielded $700, or at the rate of over $600 per ton.

In 1864, the lode passed into the hands of Eastern companies, and that part of the vein now best known was divided as follows: Bobtail Company, 433⅓ feet; Sterling Company, 66⅔ feet; Black Hawk Company, 72 feet; Field, 33⅓ feet; Trust Company, 66⅔ feet; Sensenderfer Company, 128 feet. These several properties were worked with more or less success for several years. During the two years ending September 1, 1868, the product of the Sensenderfer Company's claim was $197,155. No general and permanent success could be realized, so long as a shaft had to be sunk upon each detached piece of property, besides supporting an independent administration. One company after another suspended operations, till by the end of 1869, only the Bobtail Company continued in operation. The only hope of success was in consolidation. Since that date, through the exertions of Mr. A. N. Rogers, who has been the skillful and efficient manager of the Bobtail Company from its organization, and who is regarded as the first civil, mining, and mechanical engineer in Colorado, aided by Hon. Jerome B. Chaffee, who is one of the principal shareholders, the properties of the Sterling, Black Hawk, Trust, and Sensenderfer Companies, with one hundred feet besides, have been consolidated with the Company's property, either by purchase or stock arrangement. The Company now owns 900 feet upon this famous lode, and while producing over $200,000 per year, it has systematically and gradually been put into shape for much more extensive and profitable working.

The Bobtail tunnel, through which the mine is now worked, was completed in 1872, cutting the mine at about 500 feet in

ROBERT S. HAIGHT,

POLICE MAGISTRATE, JUSTICE OF THE PEACE,

Notary Public and City Clerk.

Collections promptly attended to.   Council Room, Black Hawk.

BONNER & FULLERTON,

ATTORNEYS AND COUNSELLORS AT LAW.

Special attention given Collecting.

Office over Hawley & Manville's,   CENTRAL CITY.

A. RITTMASTER,

—DEALER IN—

DRY GOODS AND LADIES' FURNISHING GOODS.

Ettien Block, Gregory St,   BLACK HAWK.

J. S. BUSH'S

Livery, Feed and Boarding Stable

OPPOSITE TELLER HOUSE.

Fine Saddle Horses, Carriages, and Turn-outs at low rates.

OTTERBACH & CO.,

WESTERN MARKET,

Marsh & Buffington Block, Black Hawk.

Meats, Fish, Poultry, Game and Vegetables of all Kinds. We make a specialty of Ranch Produce.

depth and 1,150 feet from the mouth. The present workings are below the tunnel level, which has been drifted the length of the property.

The main shaft is now 140 feet below the tunnel, or 640 feet below the surface. It is designed as a cage-shaft, and will be in operation as such by July 1st. The shaft is 8x16 in the clear, divided into four compartments, two for cage-ways, one bucket-way for sinking, and the remaining compartment for pump and ladder-way. Instead of two-story cages with cars for each story, holding 16 cubic feet, as on the Comstock, Mr. Rogers has constructed a one-platform cage, and will use cars holding 32 feet or about two tons. These cars will be loaded in the levels, drawn upon the cage by mules, sent to the tunnel level, and drawn by mules through the tunnel to the assorting floor, without handling.

The cars, such as have been in use for three or four years, and have stood the test to entire satisfaction, are worthy of brief description. They consist of a rectangular iron box, closed at the ends, divided for dumping in the centre, and mounted on two sets of trucks near the ends. The box or bed is hinged at the top, and is held closed at the bottom by a latch. When the car is to be dumped, the latch is quickly unfastened, the two halves part at the bottom, the hinge holds the top, the trucks roll back, and the load is dumped from the ends towards the centre.

The machinery of the mine is all underground, at the end of the main tunnel, over the mine. It consists of two large boilers, which supply steam for the hoisting machinery, pump and air compressor. The smoke-stack is built through a shaft and is 520 feet high, 250 feet of it being a three-feet-square brick stack, and the remainder an iron stack two-and-a-half feet in diameter. The hoisting machinery for the cage is as substantial as wood and iron could make it. The two drums are seven feet in diameter. Upon these are wound the flat steel wire ropes, of English manufacture, three inches in width and half an inch in thickness, with breaking strain of fifty tons, which are attached to the cages. These drums are driven by spur gear, twelve feet in diameter, and twelve-inch face. The engine driving this makes direct

—THE—
Denver Daily Times

—IS SENT TO—

CENTRAL CITY AND BLACK HAWK ON THE EVENING OF PUBLICATION.

At only 60 cents a month.   ☞ Weekly $1 25 a year.

Address, **R. W. WOODBURY**, Prop'r.

WM. GERMAIN'S
LIVERY, FEED AND SALE STABLE,

GREGORY ST., BLACK HAWK.

Elegant Turn-outs with or without drivers.

A fine carriage is kept constantly on the streets, at the service of citizens and tourists; also, will be found at the C. C. R. depot upon the arrival of trains.

DENVER BOOK STORE.

ALLEN B. SOPRIS,
Bookseller, Stationer
AND NEWS DEALER.

A Full Line of Blank Books, Letter Paper, Chromos, Fine Cutlery, Fancy Goods, Etc.

15th (F) St., P. O. Block,   *DENVER, COL.*

connection, and has reversible link motion. The sinking buckets are operated with the friction-winding drum, heretofore in use, and with a three-quarter steel wire rope of American manufacture. The pump is a direct-acting steam plunger pump, invented and patented early in 1874, by Mr. Rogers, and which has been in operation since that time. It has a capacity of 300 gallons per minute, and is suspended in such a way that it is raised by steam-winding machinery, when a line of blasts is to be fired, and lowered again ready for work, with only five minutes stoppage. The air compressor, power drills and battery in use in this mine, are described in another chapter.

The output of the mine now supplies 80 stamps, and in a short time will supply 115 stamps or 115 tons per day of mill ore. Receipts from smelting ore during 1875 averaged $5,000 per month, and it is expected they will run from $5,000 to $7,000 per month through this year.

In 1875, the Company bought the Black Hawk mill and rebuilt it internally. It contains 75 stamps of 600 ℔s. each, divided into sections of 25 stamps each, and each section has five batteries of five stamps each. Each section is run by a No. 6 Woodbury engine, so that one section may be stopped for cleaning up without interfering with the others. Power is supplied by two tubular boilers, eighteen feet long and four feet shell, the boilers and engines being attended by only one man. This rather novel plan proves to be highly satisfactory, both for convenience and economy. By careful weighing, the duty of the stamps has been determined at one ton per head per twenty-four hours. The consumption of coal to the cord is .60 to .65 of a ton per cord of ore, or about one-eleventh of a ton of coal to a ton of ore. The total cost of crushing per cord of 7 to 7½ tons, last year, was $13. By careful weighing, sampling and assaying of two lots of mill ore, one of forty and one of eighty tons, it has been determined that the average Bobtail mill ore of last year and this, assays $15 per ton, (of which about 10 per cent. is silver,) and the yield from the mill is $10 per ton or two-thirds of the assay. The other mills of the Company are the Sensenderfer mill of 20 stamps, run by steam or water, and the Eagle mill, 20 stamps, run by water

COLORADO STOCK EXCHANGE.

ORGANIZED MAY 10, 1875.

Reorganized February 2, 1876, and Incorporated under the General Laws of Colorado Territory.

Meets at 11:45 A. M. Daily, Sundays and Holidays excepted, in DENVER, COLORADO.

OFFICERS:

M. SPANGLER, President.
E. M. ASHLEY, 1st Vice President,
A. J. BEAN, 2d Vice President.
W. D. TODD, Treasurer.
E. W. COBB, Secretary.

LIST OF MEMBERS:

M. Anker,	Jere Kershaw,
James Archer,	O. E. Le Fevre,
Moritz Barth,	D. C. Lyles,
E. F. Bishop,	George C. Munson,
A. M. Cassiday,	T. Norwood,
George T. Clark,	C. E. Parker,
M. D. Clifford,	C. B. Patterson,
K. G. Cooper,	A. B. Robbins,
W. S. Collins,	George C. Roberts,
C. C. Davidson,	M. A. Shaffenburg,
J. H. Dudley,	George J. Sherman,
C. P. Elder,	George S. Smith,
Avery Gallup,	George Teal,
John R. Hambel,	Wm. D. Todd,
W. J. Kelly,	A. J. Williams.

at present, both of which have been thoroughly overhauled and refitted this year.

The production of the Bobtail mine was estimated in 1870, by Col. J. D. Hague, of the Fortieth Parallel Exploration, from statements furnished to him, at $2,500,000. Since that time, the production is known to have been very close to one million, making the total $3,500,000.

THE BUELL MINE.

This property is situated within the limits of Central City, and for the past six years has been operated by its sole owner, Hon. Bela S. Buell. It consists of 2,400 linear feet upon contiguous and connecting lodes, and has been opened by nine different shafts, varying from 500 to 100 feet in depth, all of which have been profitably worked, but only four of which are still used as working shafts. The main shaft is a vertical one, 500 feet in depth, and is now being sunk deeper, upon the Leavitt lode, and is enclosed in the large stone mill building belonging to this plant. It is substantially timbered with "sets" five feet apart, and divided into two planked compartments 2x5 feet in the clear, designed for running safety cages similar to those in the Nevada and California mines. Iron cars four feet long, two feet high, and two feet wide, holding 2,000 lbs., being loaded in any of the levels, may be run upon the cages, hoisted to the surface, and dumped in the mill with but one handling of the ore. The hoisting engine is a 70-horse power, vertical, double-cylinder engine, with link motion attachments. The hoisting machinery is calculated to sustain a strain of 40,000 lbs., and with the appliances above described, will deliver at the surface 100 tons every twelve hours. There is a third compartment in the shaft, containing the ladder-way, the steam and water-pipes connecting with the pumps. The drainage is effected by two direct-acting pumps, the first at the 300-foot level and the other at the 500-foot level. The steam-pipes are two inches in diameter, wrapped with rope to reduce condensation, and the water column four inches in diameter. The amount of water is not large, varying from 20,000 to 50,000 gallons per day. The largest pump, having a steam end 12x20, can handle the water by working one-fourth of the time, the surface water

L. C. ROCKWELL,

Attorney and Counsellor at Law,

CENTRAL CITY, COLORADO.

Office in First National Bank building.   Entrance from Eureka street.

TERRITORIAL ASSAY OFFICE,

Geo. H. Gray, Territorial Assayer.

PRACTICAL CHEMIST AND MINING ENGINEER,

Lock Box 396,   Central City, Colorado.

NATIONAL HOTEL,

LAWRENCE ST.,   -   CENTRAL CITY.

R. B. Smock, Proprietor.

☞ Transient Custom accommodated on reasonable terms. ☜

ROCKY MOUNTAIN SCENERY,

DUHEM BROS., Photographers,

NO. 448 LARIMER STREET, DENVER.

Parties wishing catalogue of Stereoscopic Views will receive the same by addressing as above.

NEW YORK STORE.

DRY GOODS, LADIES' DRESS GOODS, CARPETS, OIL-CLOTHS AND CURTAIN FIXTURES.

Harris Block, Central City.   **A. RITTMASTER.**

being conducted through a drift, which discharges several hundred feet down the gulch. The levels have been drifted fifty feet apart, and are of various lengths, those from this main shaft aggregating 4,000 feet. The ground thus far worked out on the Leavitt vein, lies mostly within 200 feet of the shaft on either side. The 300-foot level, now 700 feet in length, will be drifted 500 feet further to the west, at which point it will be 600 feet below the surface of the mountain.

This lode has an average width of six feet, widening in some places to twenty feet. The vein matter consists of a soft, white, feldspathic and quartzose rock, more or less impregnated with iron and copper pyrites. The former is classed as mill ore, and yields from $6 to $12 per ton in stamp-mill. The latter is assorted for smelting, and averages about five ounces gold and ten ounces silver per ton of 2,000 lbs., 4 per cent. copper. In 1872, 22 tons of this class of ore were shipped to Swansea, Wales, for which the consignees returned $300 per ton ; and in 1873, 250 tons were sold to the Boston & Colorado Smelting Works, at Black Hawk, for $112 per ton. With this large vein, easily worked, and the facilities for moving the ore from the mine levels to the mill, before described, together with the 60 stamps on the premises, Mr. Buell gives the cost of mining and milling at $5 per ton.

The Baxter shaft, (or discovery shaft of the Vasa,) is the next location west on this mine. It is 260 feet in depth, and in good working order. The size and characteristics of the vein at this point are similar to those at the main shaft. The next working shaft is that upon what was formerly called the "U. P. R." This shaft is 250 feet deep: At a depth of 110 feet, a level about 600 feet in length has been driven. The vein of smelting ore in this level is from 12 to 24 inches in width. The mill statement of ore from the "U. P. R.," so-called, covering a period of 18 months, shows that 6,300 tons of ore yielded 6,000 ounces of retort gold, having a fineness of 850 to 900, making the yield upward of $18 per ton, coin value. The shaft is substantially timbered, and furnished with a portable engine and hoisting works.

The next shaft is upon the Kip lode, a vein which intersects the before-mentioned lode at an angle of about 25°, at a point

Colorado Central
RAILROAD.

DENVER DIVISION—Denver to Golden, 15 Miles.

JULESBURG BRANCH—Golden Junction to Longmont via Boulder, 39 miles.

MOUNTAIN DIVISION—Golden to Black Hawk, 21 miles.

GEORGETOWN BRANCH—Forks of Clear Creek to Floyd Hill, 4 miles, (in progress to Idaho and Georgetown.)

CLEAR CREEK CANON,

TRAVERSED BY THIS LINE, IS THE MOST

Magnificent Railroad Route

IN THE WORLD.

Two trains daily to the mountain towns. The morning train from the mountains makes direct connection with the east bound Kansas Pacific Express, and leaves Denver upon the arrival of the Kansas Pacific Express.

W. A. H. LOVELAND, President.

O. H. HENRY, Superintendent.

680 feet west of the main shaft. This shaft is now 300 feet in depth, and sinking is progressing. The hoisting is done by a portable engine and ordinary hoisting machinery. This location is 1,200 feet in length, and has been extensively worked to a depth of 260 feet. The width of the vein ranges from four to eight feet, widening in one place to 22 feet, and has, of course, produced a large amount of ore. The vein matter is similar in character to the Leavitt, the streak of copper pyrites varying from four to eighteen inches in width, assaying over $100 per ton, and the mill ore yielding under stamps from $7 to $25 per ton.

Still further west upon this vein is another working shaft, 220 feet deep, called the Tallman shaft, which shows similar characteristics of vein matter.

It was early seen by Mr. Buell that these several properties constitute one property. To consolidate these once detached properties, and quiet all adverse holdings, securing government patents to the whole, was a costly undertaking, both in time and money. Having accomplished this, the entire property will ultimately be worked through the main shaft, at first described.

THE MILL.

The mill-site consists of 67,500 square feet of ground, upon which is a fire-proof stone building, 50x135 feet, besides assay office, mill office and shops. The main shaft, hoisting works and engine, occupy about one-quarter of the building, and the stamp mill, mill engine, boilers, etc., the remainder.

The mill is run by an 80-horse power engine, which also drive the Freiburg pans. The mill was erected in 1874, in the most substantial manner, and contains all the most approved appliances, both for convenience in running and gold-saving. It has 60 stamps, 30 of which are 650 ℔s. in weight, and 30 500 ℔s. in weight. The speed of the former is 25 and of the latter 30 drops per minute, falling 18 inches. The mill is divided into four sections, each having three batteries of five stamps each. The amalgamation is effected by the usual arrangement of copper plates in the batteries, and copper tables five feet wide and eight feet long. Below the tables are heavy blankets in sluices, which catch the fine

OTTO SAUER,

Wholesale and Retail Dealer in

Staple and Fancy Groceries,

Wines, Liquors and Cigars.

Tourists and Prospectors Outfitted.

JOBBING A SPECIALTY.

Main Street,   CENTRAL CITY.

GRAHAM & BALLARD,

DRUGGISTS,

—DEALERS IN—

DRUGS, MEDICINES, PAINTS, OILS,

MILL CHEMICALS,

Paper Hangings, Stationery, Fancy Goods, Etc.

(Hurlbut Brothers' old stand, Postoffice Building,)

Gregory Street,   -   BLACK HAWK.

gold that escapes amalgamation on the tables, and particles of mineral with gold attached. The blankets are washed every half-hour, and the material caught is further pulverized and then amalgamated in the Freiburg pans. Frequent tests show that by this process upon this ore, from 60 to 70 per cent. of the assay value of the ores is obtained.

Steam for the mill, hoisting engine and pumps, is supplied by three tubular boilers and two 2-flue boilers, having an aggregate capacity of 250-horse power. They are so set and arranged that they may be run separately or together. To run all the machinery requires about seven tons of coal per twenty-four hours.

As the water supply from the mine is insufficient to run the mill, a very extensive system of settling tanks has been put in outside the mill building. They are of 2-inch plank, with frame timbers 6x10 and upwards. The first tank is twenty-five feet square and four feet deep, divided into compartments 3x15. In passing from one compartment to another, the water is freed of the heavier particles and passes into a reservoir holding 80,000 gallons, which is divided into two compartments. From this it passes into the third reservoir of 100,000 gallons capacity, and from this it runs into a large cistern under the mill floor, from which it is elevated to the mill and boiler tanks, sufficiently clear for use. In the settling arrangements, the water travels 400 feet. Besides the tanks described, there is another reservoir of 250,000 gallons capacity, making, with the race-ways, a total tank capacity of 500,000 gallons.

The entire cost of the surface improvements upon this mine exceeds $100,000, and this, with the purchase of contiguous mines and quieting adverse claims, has been furnished from the profits of the mine without outside capital. The entire product of the whole mine, made up as carefully as circumstances will admit, is about $1,000,000. Of this amount, nearly $500,000 has been produced from 400 feet contiguous to the main shaft, in a little more than three years' working.

BURROUGHS LODE.

This is one of the earliest discoveries and most prominent lodes in the county. It is situated on Quartz Hill, 150 to 200

ALVIN MARSH,
ATTORNEY AT LAW,
BLACK HAWK, COLORADO.

Office in Marsh & Buffington's brick block.

ED. C. HUGHES'
"LITTLE MARKET,"
Gregory Street, Black Hawk,

Is always well-supplied with the finest Meats, Game, Fish and Vegetables to be found in the market.

H. P. COWENHOVEN,
GROCER,

Gregory Street, - *BLACK HAWK.*

COLORADO HOUSE
S. D. QUAINTANCE, Proprietor,

Main Street, - *Black Hawk, Colorado.*

Best Accommodations in the City.

BLACK HAWK BREWERY.
Samuel Haubrich,

Manufacturer of Lager Beer. Saloons, Restaurants and Families Supplied on short notice.

feet above the bed of Nevada gulch. Its course is north 85° east, true, and its dip south from 10° to 15° from a vertical line. The country rock is the same as that throughout the county, half gneissic and half granitic. The size of the vein is less than that of most of the noted lodes, rarely ever reaching more than three or four feet in width. The vein matter may be characterized, in comparison with other famous lodes, as a high grade mill ore. The proportion of smelting ore to mill ore is probably not more than 1 to 50. It contains from $100 to $150 per ton in gold and silver, and carries no remunerative per cent. of copper.

The lode has been opened and worked a distance of over 2,500 feet. Like all of the earlier discoveries, it was pre-empted in claims of one hundred feet each, and in 1863 and '64 a dozen mining companies were organized upon Burroughs lode property, leaving several hundred feet unsold! A map of the lode, made in 1869, shows thirty shafts of various depths upon 2,300 feet of this lode. Of course such mining as this has been at an immense disadvantage, and if the whole property had uniformly paid even expenses, it would have been a guarantee that this was the best lode in the mountains.

Ophir.—This is the oldest company organized on Burroughs property, if not the oldest in the county. The property on this lode consists of 462 feet, including the discovery claim, and is the same as the Pat Casey claim that paid so largely in 1861 and '62, but of which we have no data. The only subsequent data now obtainable, are those furnished by Col. George E. Randolph. During five months of his superintendency, beginning in April, 1868, there were mined 2,437 tons of ore which yielded $45,567, an average of $28.70 per ton. The prices then paid were $52.50 per foot for sinking main shaft, $12 to $20 per foot for drifting, and from $25 to $50 per fathom for stoping. The two shafts were then about 600 feet deep, the pump shaft being furnished with an 8-inch Cornish pump. The data further shows that every fathom of ground stoped produced seven and six-tenths tons, or about one cord of milling and smelting ore. The total production of the mine for the years 1867 and '68, was $171,568.67. In 1869, some mining was done under leases, producing $25,541.55.

WM. EDMUNDSON,

Physician,

Central City, - Colorado.

Office in the First National Bank building, on Eureka Street.

W. H. JACKSON, D. D.'S.,

Main Street, Central City, Col.

ALL DENTAL OPERATIONS PERFORMED WITH CARE.

Office over Hanington & Mellor's Bank.

L. C. TOLLES,
PHYSICIAN AND SURGEON,

CENTRAL CITY, COLORADO.

Can be found at his office in Mullen Block, Main Street, when not professionally engaged.

R. G. ADUDDELL, M. D.,
SURGEON,

Office--First door below John Best's Pharmacy.

CENTRAL CITY, COLORADO.

L. L. RATLIFF, M. D.
PHYSICIAN,

Gregory Street, - - BLACK HAWK.

Office opposite the Postoffice.

From that time the mine remained idle, or nearly so, until May, 1873, when it was leased by Messrs. Roberts & Co. The mine was full of water, out of repair, and no large amount of ore developed. Several months were spent in draining the mine, and putting it in producing order, so that not until January, 1874, had they received back the money so expended. From that time to the expiration of the lease, April 1, 1875, the work was very profitable. The production of mill ore during their lease amounted to 554⅜ cords, or about 3,600 tons, which produced 5,005.58 ounces retort gold, that sold for $104,007.24, currency, an average of $28.61, currency, or $26 coin per ton. During this period, 162 tons of smelting ore were sold, from which was realized $18,739.20, making a total production of $122,746.44. The proportion of smelting ore to the mill ore was as 1 to 21.6, and the average receipts for smelting ore per ton, $115.67.

Upon the expiration of the Roberts lease, the mine was leased for a term of years to D. Sullivan & Co., who also have leases of adjoining ground. The main shaft has been sunk to the depth of 1,000 feet, the deepest shaft in Colorado. The new lessees are doing considerable dead work, and of course spending more money than they receive. No one who knows the property, however, which first and last has produced three-quarters of a million dollars, doubts that the enterprising lessees will ultimately extract a large profit from the mine.

It is worthy of notice, by way of contrast, that the last 160 feet of this shaft have been sunk for $15 per foot, as against $52.50 in 1868.

The properties of the Gilpin, Colorado, Burroughs, and La Crosse companies, and W. H. Cushman on the east, and of the First National, Gold Hill, Baltimore, and Quartz Hill companies on the west of the Ophir property, have been worked to depths ranging from 100 to 500 feet, but the writer possesses no data of total production or yield per ton. A profit will never be realized by working them as detached properties. Consolidation is the only road to success.

Rocky Mountain News

ESTABLISHED APRIL, 1859.

The Oldest, Largest, Cheapest and Best Newspaper between the Missouri River and California.

Weekly News, 40 Columns, $3 per year; $1.75 six months; $1 three months.
Daily News, 36 Columns, $10 per year, by mail, or $1 per month.

JOB PRINTING AND BLANK BOOK MANUFACTURING OF ALL KINDS.

Address, WM. N. BYERS, Denver.

M. H. ROOT,

Contractor and Builder in

STONE AND BRICK WORK

CENTRAL CITY, COLORADO.

Also, Building of Furnaces, Excavating, Moving Mill Machinery, Etc.

Residence on Eureka Street.   P. O. Box 266.

L. C. SNYDER,

—DEALER IN—

HAY, CORN, OATS, CHOPPED FEED,

Horses, Mules, and Wagons.

Will also contract for the hauling of quartz and all kinds of mining machinery. Mine timbers furnished at reasonable rates.

Stone Fire-proof, Gregory Street,   BLACK HAWK.

KANSAS LODE.

This great mother vein, known and worked about 3,500 feet in extent, outcropping on the northern slope of Quartz Hill, was one of the early discoveries of 1859. It was worked for surface ores with excellent results, but on reaching the pyrites work was abandoned, and not resumed with any marked success until 1869. So doubtful was its value and so difficult was the treatment of the ore, that it is believed that in 1866 nearly every claim on the lode could have been bought for $5,000. With better milling and an opportunity to sell the best ore to the smelting works, work was resumed at several points in 1869, since which time it has been very productive. The late Mr. B. C. Waterman was the first to work vigorously and systematically, upon what has since been known as the

Waterman-Kansas—a property consisting of 300 feet. He encountered an extended pinch, and failed to reach the body of rich ore which he was confident lay below. Subsequently, the property was leased to Mr. J. C. Fagan, and on December 25th, 1873, Dennis Sullivan, Esq., was placed in charge as manager. We are kindly permitted to publish the results of seventeen and a half months' working, ending June 10, 1875.

RECEIPTS.

From mill gold sold,	$ 112,032 03
" smelting ore,	5,265 44
" tribute work,	3,875 65
" earnings of mill,	6,593 62
Total,	$127,766 74

EXPENDITURES.

For contracts,	$ 22,482 96	
" days' labor,	12,730 67	
" hauling and crushing,	5,661 00	
" mill expenses,	25,262 38	
" other expenses	18,561 27	84,698 28
Net profit,		$ 43,068 46

The average contract prices paid, were for sinking shaft, $15 per foot; drifting, $4.50 per foot, and for stoping, $11 to $15 per fathom. The average yield of the mill ore was $12.50 per ton, and of the smelting ore, $60 to $75 per ton. Since that

BELFORD & REED,
ATTORNEYS AND COUNSELLORS AT LAW,
CENTRAL CITY, COLORADO.

Office in First National Bank building. Entrance on Eureka St.

CENTRAL CITY BREWERY
AND BOARDING HOUSE,

Eureka Street, - - *Central City, Col.*

WM. LEHMKUHL, Proprietor.

TOLL GATE MARKET.
BLACK HAWK, COLORADO,

Fresh and Salt Meats, Fish, Poultry, Game and Vegetables in their season.

REMINE & WEISS, Proprietors.

MOUNTAIN HOUSE,
BLACK HAWK, COLORADO.

The Table is supplied with the best the market affords. Omnibus to and from all trains.

P. B. WRIGHT, - Proprietor.

J. R. MORGAN,
Carriage and Wagon Manufactory

Spring Street, Central City.

BLACKSMITHING AND HORSESHOEING A SPECIALTY.

time the three hundred feet of ground lying west of this property, formerly called the Whitcomb claims, and latterly the Monmouth-Kansas, has been worked through the Waterman-Kansas shaft, and comparatively little development has been done in the Waterman property. An 8-inch Cornish pump has been put in at a cost of $8,000, which is doing good work. The shaft is now 600 feet deep, and the whole property in excellent condition for working. Recently, the Waterman and Monmouth properties have been consolidated, making 600 consecutive feet, which will in future be worked as one property.

Monmouth-Kansas.—Mr. D. Sullivan's management of this property commenced July 15, 1875. As stated, it consists of 300 feet, immediately adjoining the Waterman property on the west. By favor we are permitted to give the monthly production, expenses, and profit from July 15, 1875, to April 15, 1876.

	Receipts.	Expenses.	Profit.
To July 15, 1875,	$ 2,448 17	$ 1,649 71	$ 798 46
" Aug. " "	6,453 42	3,136 86	3,316 56
" Sept. " "	7,372 99	3,515 85	3,857 14
" Oct. " "	5,110 30	3,010 30	2,100 00
" Nov. " "	7,972 85	4,036 70	3,936 15
" Dec. " "	11,230 92	6,770 89	4,460 03
" Jan. " 1876,	8,921 85	4,611 37	4,310 48
" Feb. " "	7,273 37	5,258 46	2,014 91
" Mch. " "	7,675 00	5,439 54	2,235 46
" Apr. " "	5,970 91	3,225 11	2,754 80
Totals,	$70,438 78	$40,654 79	$29,783 99

It will be observed that the profit is forty-two and fourteen one-hundreths per cent. of the gross proceeds.

First National Kansas.—This property consists of 450 feet lying east and adjoining the Waterman property. The only data of yield we are able to give, are those produced by Wheeler & Co., under lease from March, 1871, to January, 1872, a period of ten months. The product was

From sale of mill gold,	- - - - -	$ 68,829 34
" " smelting ore,	- - - -	9,382 16
Total	- - - - - - -	$78,211 50

Henry Thompson,

—DEALER IN ALL KINDS OF—

FURNITURE

—AND—

UPHOLSTERED GOODS.

Also, a full and complete stock of the latest styles of

Burial Cases and Caskets,

BOTH WOOD AND METALLIC.

Special attention given to embalming and shipping or keeping bodies, having a Corpse Preserver for the latter purpose.

N. B.—I give personal attention to all undertaking entrusted to my care.

EXPENSES.

Mining expenses,	$ 23,760 62	
Milling,	23,844 00	
Rental,	12,779 81	60,384 43

Net profit, - - - - - - - $17,827 07

Had they been the owners of the property and treated their ore in their own mill, which can now be done at an expense of $18 per cord, their profits would have been increased as follows: Rental, $12,779.81; extra cost of milling, $12,504; making a difference of $25,283, or a net profit of $43,110.88.

English-Kansas.—This property is situated nearly a half-mile east of the properties above mentioned, but on the same great vein. Our statement covers a period of nineteen consecutive months, including both the working by the lessees, Messrs. Gray, Bennett & Root, and by the English Company, after the purchase. During that time, Messrs. Thatcher, Standley & Co. purchased the mill gold produced, which amounted to 4,948 ozs. 18 dwt. 12 gr., retort gold, at an average price of $18.43 per ounce, or $91,074.75, currency. Tribute working was also pursued by the English Company, of which there is no account extant. During the same period 379 tons of smelting ore were sold, of which the average assay was $72.42, aggregating an assay value of $27,449.18.

Ophir-Kansas—Consists of 200 feet on the Kansas lode. The only data of production at hand are those returned to the company by Roberts & Co., lessees, from May 1871, to November, 1873. The production for that period was $86,730, of which $4,780.62 was received for smelting ore.

Alger-Kansas.—This east extension of the Kansas vein was discovered by William Alger in September, 1859, and thus antedates all other records on this vein east of No. 6 east on the Kansas proper. For seven or eight years it was worked more or less, and in 1867 a large body of ore 22 feet in width was worked, yielding from three to seven ounces per cord. Recently, Jacob Tascher, the owner of this property, resumed work with success, the ore running from two to seven and a half ounces per cord. The Central City tunnel, just started, will cut the lode at a depth of 75 feet near the centre of the property.

Henry Hanington. John Mellor.

HANINGTON & MELLOR,

BANKERS

CENTRAL CITY, COL.

Do a General Banking Business.

COLLECTIONS PROMPTLY ATTENDED TO.

BATES LODE.

This lode was discovered by Gregory on the 19th of May, 1859. It was located by Captain William H. Bates, who deeded Gregory one-half of the discovery claim. The balance of the lode was taken by Captain Packard, Judge Slaughter, Captain Sopris and others. The pay dirt on the surface yielded by sluicing, an average of $20 per day to the hand for months together, and they frequently obtained from a single flour sack full of choice dirt from $50 to $75.

The lode furnished the basis for the organization of several mining companies. The Union Company purchased Nos. 1 and 2 west. During sixteen consecutive months, beginning in 1866 and ending in 1868, these claims produced $205,000. Owing to litigation this mine has lain idle until recently. The owners claim there is $100,000 worth of ore in sight. Smelting ore now being mined, is worth delivered in Denver, $240 per ton. There are about 250 tons of ore of high smelting grade, piled upon the premises, awaiting the result of litigation. The depth of the main shaft is 410 feet.

The Bates & Baxter Company's property, consisting of Nos. 1, 2 and 3, east, has also produced largely, particularly claim No. 1. In January and February, 1864, 81 cords of ore yielded 1,092 ounces of gold, and the production was large for several months. The property has been idle since 1865. The main shaft is 380 feet deep.

The Rocky Mountain Company own 250 feet on the Bates where it crosses Gregory gulch. This property has been worked to a depth of 175 feet. The company's capital was chiefly expended in surface improvements.

The Bates-Hunter, west of the gulch, has paid largely and is a good mine. Westward, the lode has been worked in a desultory way, but sufficient to show that it is good property. It is believed the total production of the lode, could it be ascertained, would reach, if not exceed, half a million dollars.

Illinois Mine.—This mine is situated on the south slope of Quartz Hill, and embraces 1,000 feet upon the Illinois lode, and 1,400 feet on the Confidence, the two being identical for 400 feet from the west end of the property. In early times, 310 feet upon the Illinois, belonging to one party, was very

Hendrie Bros. & Bolthoff,

CENTRAL CITY, COLORADO,

Manufacturers of all kinds of

MINING MACHINERY.

WET AND DRY PULVERIZERS.

IMPROVED PORTABLE HOISTING & PUMPING ENGINES.

AGENTS FOR

**KNOWLES' STEAM MINING AND FEED PUMPS,
HALLIDIE'S WIRE TRAMWAY,
ROOT'S BLOWERS, BLAKE CRUSHERS,
FRIEDMAN INJECTORS,
STEAM JET PUMPS, ETC., ETC.**

successfully worked to a depth of 200 feet. From 1867 to 1869, this part of the lode was operated by a Chicago company, and managed by Mr. George R. Mitchell, during which time the extensive surface improvements were made upon the mine and considerable underground work done, principally from the proceeds of the mine. The present owners, Messrs. Buell, Woods & Jacobs, have purchased additional ground, and now hold patents for both lodes and two mill sites.

The main shaft is 230 feet deep, and is furnished with a Cornish self-dumping skip, arranged for hoisting both ore and water, carrying 20 cubic feet at a load. The bucket shaft is 180 feet deep, and about 90 feet west of the main shaft. The lateral development consists of a level drifted east from the bucket shaft to a distance of 555 and a depth of 160 feet. The 200-foot level has been drifted west to the end of the property about 140 feet, and westward about 200 feet from the skip shaft. A large portion of the ground is stoped out above the lower level east of the skip shaft, showing a vein averaging from two to three feet, sometimes widening to ten feet. The yield of the stamp rock for thirty-four weeks in the summer of 1868, was as follows: 1,500 tons yielded 1,538 ozs. retort bullion, worth $15.50 coin, or $15.88 per ton, coin value. During this time 42 tons of smelting ore were sold, of which the assay was $108 per ton in gold and silver. The minerals in this mine consist of iron and copper pyrites, associated with some zinc blende and galena. The gangue is a soft rock, requiring comparatively little blasting.

The surface improvements consist of extensive frame buildings, connected and covering both shafts, the engine, boiler, hoisting works, a 22-stamp mill, blacksmith shop and office. The engine is a horizontal one, $15\frac{1}{2}$x36 cylinder, supplied by steam from a tubular boiler 14 feet by 52 inches. The hoisting machinery is very substantial, capable of raising 100 tons per day. The frictional winding-drum operating the skip, was designed by Mr. A. N. Rogers. A line of shafting, resting upon stone pillar blocks, transmits power to the bucket shaft, hoister, and to the mill. Tram-ways are laid from the skip shaft to the mill; also in the levels. The cost of the

The Colorado Transcript,

PUBLISHED WEEKLY, AT

GOLDEN, - COLORADO.

GEO. WEST, Editor and Proprietor.

THE TRANSCRIPT is devoted to the Farming, Mining and Manufacturing interests of the country. Being located at the smelting and manufacturing centre of a large scope of country, it will be found indispensable to those interested in these industries.

Terms:--$3.00 per annum, in advance.

Blacksmith and Wagon Shop,

LEITZMAN & BOELLERT, Proprietors,

MAIN STREET, - BLACK HAWK.

—ALSO, DEALERS IN—

AGRICULTURAL IMPLEMENTS OF ALL KINDS.

Mine and Mill Repairing done on short notice.

Cold, Soft Spring Water.

Hotels, Restaurants and Private Families Supplied with Cold, Clear, Soft Spring Water.

Having the finest Springs, and an abundant supply of Water THE YEAR ROUND, I can fill all orders on short notice.

JACOB TASCHER.

improvements made by the Chicago company, exceeded $100,000, and were of so substantial a character that for the most part they remain in good order.

This property has been worked during the past year, producing mill ore that averaged $15.50 per ton, coin value, and smelting ore for which $100 per ton, currency, was paid by the Boston & Colorado Smelting Works.

St. Louis.—Situated on the east end of Gunnell hill, west of Central. This lode was discovered in 1860 by William Daley, and ever since has been the standing example of a class of lodes, having very rich ore, but in which the gold is so coated with a "rust" or an "oxide," or a something else, as to render amalgamation by the ordinary means very difficult, if not impossible. The surface dirt was exceedingly rich, and many a hard-up prospector has panned out a grub-stake from it. The writer saw $15 washed out of an oyster-can full of dirt just as it came from the pocket. Seven hundred feet of this lode came near being sold to a Boston party for $30,000, but happily escaped, else it might not now be on the list of large producers. In 1872, Messrs. A. & F. Kilbourn purchased Nos. 1 and 2 west, and in August, 1874, formed a copartnership with Eastern men under the firm name of F. Kilbourn & Co. Two adjoining claims are leased, and the 400 feet of the vein will be worked through the same shaft. The shaft is now 250 feet deep. The best yield obtained from the time Kilbourn & Co. commenced work to the spring of 1876, was at the Kimber Mill, five cords yielding five and a half ounces per cord. Since that time the ore has been running much higher, reaching 20 ounces per cord in gold from the coppers, and by panning the material left in the batteries, four ounces per cord were added, making 24 ounces or $55 per ton. During the past two months $1,500 in gold has been taken from blanketings and ground and amalgamated in pans. Thirty-six dollars were taken out of 80 ℔s. of blanketings. From $3\frac{1}{2}$ to $8\frac{1}{2}$ ounces has been the yield from a barrel of blanket tailings. The mass of ore producing these yields is eight to nine feet wide, and has already produced $5,600. Two men in the mine, with two on top, lately produced in one week, an amount of ore that yielded $1,070. Previous to

WOOD'S PATENT

Steam or Pneumatic

ROCK DRILLS

Manufactured by the HEWES & PHILLIPS WORKS, Newark, N. J.

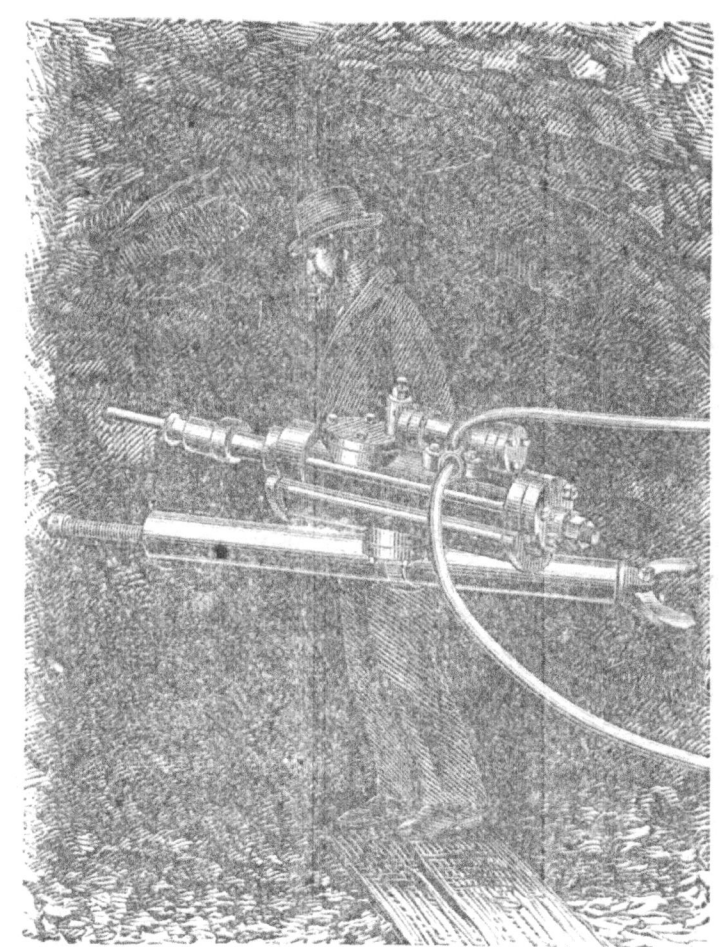

Used in the BOBTAIL, CARIBOU and CONSOLIDATED VIRGINIA.

Hendrie Bros. & Bolthoff,

AGENTS,

Central City, - Colorado.

reaching this body of rich ore, Messrs. Kilbourn & Co. had run about 80 cords, averaging 4½ ounces per cord, leaving nearly as much more upon the dump. Should the Fryer Company wish to try their process in Colorado, we commend the St. Louis ore as the "worst in the business."

Pleasant View.—Located on the east end of Gunnell hill, and consists of 1,200 feet. The books of the First National Bank of Central and its predecessors, show that during the management of Mr. E. C. Beach, former proprietor of the mine, $42,718 from this mine passed through that bank. The average yield of the mill rock was about $20 per ton, and the profit upon the whole working more than 50 per cent. of the production. The vein is large in the shaft, and the character of the ore similar to that of the New Foundland and St. Louis. Some of the ore assays very high—two to three thousand dollars per ton. During this year the mine has passed into the hands of a home company, organized under the laws of Colorado. The mine has been thoroughly retimbered, and suitable steam hoisting works erected upon the property. The shaft is now 230 feet deep, and work is regularly progressing. At a depth of 150 feet, a level has been run 150 feet west and 65 feet east. At present the yield is from 4½ to 5 ounces per cord.

O. K. Lode.—This lode is situated on Mammoth Hill, and is considered to be the western extension of the Leavitt. It is 1,500 feet in length, and patented. Mr. James Hanna, the present owner, has sunk the main shaft to a depth of 178 feet, and proposes to continue. Forty-five feet of drifting has been done, but no stoping. It is Mr. Hanna's intention to open the mine extensively before any work for profit is begun. The ore from the shaft has averaged 4½ ounces per cord, or $9.84 per ton under stamps. Of a lot of ore containing ten tons, eight tons (one cord) were sent to stamp mill, and yielded five ounces gold, which sold for $87.50; deducting hauling and milling, $27.50, the net receipts were $50, or $6.25 per ton. The remaining two tons were sent to Collom's Concentration Works, and assayed $37 per ton, 37 per cent. sulphides, and a little copper. The price paid per ton was $15.95; deducting 70c per ton for hauling, the net receipts were $16.25 per ton,

First National Bank
OF DENVER.

---o---

DESIGNATED DEPOSITORY OF THE UNITED STATES.

---o---

Authorized Capital, $500,000.

Paid-in Capital, $200,000. Surplus, $200,000.

---o---

Transact a General Banking Business.

---o---

J. B. CHAFFEE, President.
  W. S. CHEESMAN, Vice President.
    D. H. MOFFAT, JR., Cashier.
      G. W. KASSLER, Assistant Cashier.

---o---

Corner Sixteenth and Larimer,   **DENVER, COL.**

a difference of $10 per ton in favor of concentration on this class of ore. The smelting ore assays $90 per ton.

The O. K. vein averages three feet in width, and the sinking, including the cost of timbering, costs $17 per foot.

Satisfaction.—Situated on Pine street, Central. This is a relocation of an abandoned property, owned and operated by the estate of J. H. Hense, John Scudder, S. I. Lorah, and Dr. W. H. Jackson. A very large, easily worked vein, that at present yields only about $6 per ton. The shaft is 180 feet deep. Steam hoisting works will be put upon this property in August of this year.

Bugher.—Claims Nos. 2 and 3 east, are worked by Joseph Hafer & Co. The ground has been worked out to the depth of 100 feet, producing 300 cords that averaged five ounces per cord; or, reduced to tons and dollars, 2,100 tons yielding $12.50 per ton.

Bull-of-the-Woods.—Situated on Central City hill, also worked by Joseph Hafer. Two hundred feet of the lode are opened to the depth of 60 feet. The vein is small, but rich, yielding by stamps, $25 per ton. Forty-two tons yielded $1,800, or about $43 per ton.

Gettysburg.—This lode is on Bates hill, and is owned by Jos. Hafer and the Briggs Bros. The ground of the former is leased to John Eads & Co. The shaft is 125 feet deep. The ore from this mine has yielded seven ounces per cord, or about $17 per ton under stamps, 40 cords having produced 280 ounces. The Briggs Bros.' ground, lying to the west, is leased to Westover & Co., who are taking out six-ounce ore.

Alaska.—Situated in Enterprise district, and formerly worked by Messrs. Belden & Tennal. Now owned and operated by W. H. Bush & Co. This lode so far as worked, to the depth of 149 feet, has been noted for ore rich in lead, often reaching 72 per cent., with only $18 in silver. Under recent operations the ore has brought as high as $40 per ton.

Chihuahua.— Located in Enterprise district, 1,500 feet, patented. A vein of great width, carrying iron and copper pyrites in bands, running through the vein matter. Assays show the average value at about $75 per ton, of which one-half

COLORADO
Dressing and Smelting Company

CAPITAL, $250,000.

WILLIAM HANCOCK, Pres't,	Trenton, N. J.
DANIEL PETERS, Vice Pres't,	" "
PETER W. CROZER, Sec. and Treas.,	" "
JOHN COLLOM, Gen'l Manager,	Golden, Col.

EASTERN OFFICE, TRENTON, N. J.

WESTERN OFFICE, GOLDEN, COL.

BUYS, CONCENTRATES AND SMELTS
GOLD, SILVER, COPPER and LEAD ORES.

CONCENTRATING WORKS AT IDAHO SPRINGS,
Capacity, 75 Tons a Day.

CONCENTRATING WORKS AT BLACK HAWK,
Capacity, 100 Tons a Day.

SMELTING WORKS AT GOLDEN,
Capacity, 30 Tons a Day.

100-Ton Concentrating Works to be built at Georgetown and Boulder.

is silver. Selected samples from this mine have assayed 1,900 ounces in silver. The lode is developed by a shaft 97 feet in depth, and by a tunnel on the vein, commencing in Little Missouri gulch, and running east, now 177 feet in length, and in progress. This very promising mine is owned by W. H. Bush & Co.

Lewis.—Situated on Quartz hill, and considered to be the east extension of the Burroughs vein, which it strongly resembles. Developed by one shaft 115 feet deep, one 85 feet, and two 35 feet each. The mill ore has averaged 5½ ounces per cord, through the season. The vein is from twenty-two inches to six feet in width, carrying iron and copper pyrites, the former containing most of the gold. This mine is owned by W. H. Bush & Co., who have 800 feet patented, and hold 700 feet additional by location.

First Centennial.—This lode is owned by Robert S. Haight and L. C. Miley, situated on the south side of Chase gulch, below the Belden & Tennal tunnel. They have shafts on the vein at the respective depths of 80, 40, 45, 40, and 40 feet, showing in many places an 8-foot vein. The mill rock runs from eight to twenty-five ounces per cord (of six tons) in stamp mill.

Mountain City.—Owned by C. C. Miller and others. Has been worked more or less since its discovery in 1865, with good results. During 1875, two men, who had a lease of a part of the property, took out of the mine by their own labor, over $5,000. At the present time the property is leased to three different parties, the mill ore running from two to eleven ounces per cord, or from $5 to $28 per ton, and the smelting ore from $45 to $250 per ton.

Cashier.—Situated near the lake, and owned by Mr. J. W. Holman. While sinking the shaft 90 feet deep, 434 tons of ore were produced, yielding $4,123, or $9.50 per ton. Several tons of smelting ore were also obtained, assaying over $500 per ton.

Spinney.—This is one of the small but very rich lodes of the county, situated near the Justice, in Lake district. It has been worked to the depth of 85 feet, and opened by numerous

J. ALDEN SMITH,

(Territorial Geologist,)

Examiner of Mines, Mineralogist and Assayer.

Offices at Sunshine and Boulder.

Will examine and report upon mines of Gold, Silver, Copper and other minerals in all parts of the State. Samples for assay can be sent by mail, and will receive prompt attention.

GOLDEN
Foundry & Machine Shop

With new and improved machinery, I am prepared to execute,
at short notice,

Repairs of Steam Engines, Boilers, Stamp Mills, Etc.

Particular attention given to making

PULVERIZERS, CORNISH ROLLERS, LOAM AND DRY
SAND CASTINGS, FOR METALLURGISTS.

Iron and Brass Castings.   **Cash paid for Old Iron.**

SILAS BERTENSHAW.

"TEMPLE OF FASHION,"

MAIN STREET, CENTRAL CITY.

*Dry Goods, Clothing, Ladies' Furnishing Goods,
Carpets and Oil-cloths.*

PRICES ALWAYS REASONABLE.

B. W. WISEBART.

shafts for 1,500 feet. The mill dirt has run from nine to twenty-eight ounces, usually approaching the latter figure. The smelting ore is worth about $63 per ton, and contains a large percentage of silver. The vein is from six to twenty-two inches in width. Owned and worked by Darius Pippin and others.

J. P. Whitney.—Situated on south side of Eureka gulch. Leased in February last to Hinman & Sears. They have sunk the shaft 70 feet, and are drifting and stoping. The pay crevice is 20 inches wide, of which 14 inches are galena, worth $30 per ton, the remainder, mill dirt, yielding about $10 per ton.

Bowker.—In Nevada district, owned by L. A. Johnson, and leased by Casbàum & Co. The main shaft is 295 feet deep. The ore is galena and copper pyrites, assaying one ounce in gold, twenty-eight ounces silver, and forty per cent. lead, and is sold at Young & West's, Golden.

Jones.—This is the "Kentuck" lode of 1859. Nos. 3 and 4 west, owned by Daniel McGonigal, are leased and in operation by John Cox. The shaft on this property is 250 feet deep, and westward the ground has been stoped out, the mill dirt for two years averaging 13 ozs. 14 dwts. per cord, or about $30 per ton, and the smelting ore bringing from $32 to $94 per ton. The ore is iron pyrites and zinc blende. Work is now progressing westward with good results.

Hubert.—Situated in Nevada district, upon the same vein as the Suderberg. The shaft on No. 2 west is 300 feet deep. Three levels have been drifted aggregating over 400 feet, and 100 feet east of the shaft a winze has been sunk from the 110 to the 240-foot level, opening a large body of good ground. The vein is from two to five feet in width, consisting of galena, zinc blende, and iron pyrites. In April and May, 350 tons were sold to Collom's Dressing Works, at prices varying from $5 to $16 per ton, averaging $8, which was more than could be obtained from stamp mill. In the latter part of May, the mine was producing 35 tons per day, and yielding under stamps $11.80 per ton. The smelting ore brings $27 per ton.

THE DENVER TRIBUNE,

(DAILY AND WEEKLY,)

Has the largest circulation and the most reading matter of any paper in Colorado.

Daily, 32 columns, by mail, $10 per year; Weekly, 36 columns, $3 per year.

BEST ADVERTISING MEDIUM IN THE TERRITORY.

First-class Bindery and Job Printing Department connected.

HERMAN BECKURTS, Proprietor.

P. O. Box 351. Established in 1867.

JAMES BURRELL,

U. S. Commissioner, Notary Public and Conveyancer.

FIRE INSURANCE IN NATIONAL BOARD COMPANIES.

Patents obtained to Mines, Adverse Claims Filed, U. S. Titles to Town Lots obtained or contested. Mines, Stores and Houses bought, sold or leased.

Office in H. M. Burrell's Drug Store,   *CENTRAL CITY.*

N. H. McCall.   Oscar Lewis.

McCALL & LEWIS,

HAY, GRAIN AND COAL DEALERS,

PROPRIETORS CENTRAL TRANSFER LINE.

Lawrence Street,   *CENTRAL CITY.*

Mark goods care McCall & Lewis.

Borton and Roderick Dhu.—These two celebrated locations upon the same vein, which have been so productive in the past, are about to be consolidated—so it is reported—making 2,200 linear feet owned and worked by a new company. The deepest shaft on this property is, we believe, 550 feet, and it is claimed—probably truly—that over $600,000 have been taken from this lode.

Kent County.—This is one of the old discoveries of 1859; 1,296 feet west of discovery claim being worked by Mr. Joseph B. Tomlinson. The main shaft is 400 feet deep, and two others are 100 and 110 respectively. Four levels are being run from the main shaft, at 150, 220, 300 and 400 feet, respectively, from surface. The mill rock is treated at custom mills at Black Hawk, and yields an average of seven ounces per cord, or about $17.50 per ton. From 14 to 20 tons per day are sent to mill. The smelting ore runs from $113 to $125 per ton. Mr. Tomlinson estimates that this lode has produced, since its discovery, nearly $1,000,000.

The prices of work paid at this mine are, sinking, $10 to $12, shaft 5x9; drifting, $3 to $4 per foot; back-stoping, $11 to $18 per fathom.

IDLE PROPERTY.

Among lodes of first class reputation, but which are now idle for a variety of causes, the following may be mentioned as examples:

New Foundland.—Situated half way from Central to Nevada. Main shaft 375 feet deep. The lode was opened upon a very wide body or chimney of ore, of high grade, which continued to the depth of a hundred feet or more, below which the vein is of ordinary dimensions, averaging four feet. For the last 100 feet the vein of paying ore has been pinched, but yielded smelting ore worth $100 per ton, and mill dirt that ran from three to five ounces per cord. The production is not definitely known, but a careful compilation of such data as can be obtained, shows that $50,000 can be traced to the parties who have worked it.

Caledonia.—Situated in Hawkeye district, near Wide Awake. Discovered in 1860. Main shaft 267 feet, well timbered.

Hawley & Manville,

―――GENERAL DEALERS IN―――

Groceries and Provisions,

Crockery, Glassware, Woodenware,

HAY AND GRAIN,

POWDER, FUSE,

FURNITURE.

Canned Meats of every description, especially for Tourists.

MAIN STREET, CENTRAL CITY.

Five other shafts from 40 to 140 feet deep. Claim No. 1 west has produced $56,000. No data extant of the production of other claims. Surface ore yielded from six to ten ounces per cord, and upon pyritous ore, ran as high as 30 ounces per cord, not falling below 18 ounces per cord from July to November, 1861. The gold from this claim is .850 fine, and allowing 7½ tons per cord, the yield for nearly four consecutive months was from $27 to $68 per ton. At a depth of 100 feet a pinch was encountered in the shaft, which continued without a pocket of any value for 160 feet. When work was suspended in 1865, there was every indication that the pinch was passed. A vein of pyrites of iron was reached that assays $52 per ton, and that in sinking three feet increased from a mere marker to ten inches in width. Other claims have been worked since that produced well, but no figures are at hand.

Parent.—Situated on the summit of the hill south of the Gregory. Discovered in 1864 by Sid. Parent, who worked it during that summer. At a depth of 35 feet, the ore yielded in Cheney's mill, Lake gulch, from 25 to 26½ ounces per cord, or from $70 to $75 per ton. Subsequently, the ore decreased in quality, until only two ounces per cord could be obtained, and at a depth of 220 feet work was suspended. Probably, a few thousand dollars expended in sinking would restore this property to its former comparative rank. II. H. Atkins, Esq., of Georgetown, is the owner. The

Gardner, California, Hidden Treasure, and *Indiana* are all locations upon one vein, in Nevada district, covering 2,500 to 3,000 feet in length. The vein is a strong one, varying from three to twelve feet, and is cheaply worked. The ore is iron and copper pyrites, with some galena and zinc blende intermixed. The proportion of smelting ore is not large, and the assays of lots sold vary from three ounces gold and eleven ounces silver per ton, to four of gold and twenty of silver. The mill ore, however, is large in amount, and is uniformly of high milling grade.

That part of the Gardner known as the Clark-Gardner has been worked to a depth of 400 feet, and has averaged largely, the mill ore averaging $12 to $14 per ton.

COLLINS' DOOR STOP.

This invention consists of a rubber-headed bolt, A, sliding in a casing and acted upon by a spiral spring which forces it downward. To the upper end of the bolt is pivoted a lever rod connected to a crank. When the latter is carried below its pivot, the spring is free to act and so to cause the bolt to hold the door. When it is desired to throw the device out of action, the crank is raised above the pivot, and is carried by the spring against the stop pin, B, when it holds the bolt securely in elevated position. The invention is easily applied, and in case of the spring becoming weakened by use, a new one is readily inserted.

State and County Rights For Sale.

Address, COLLINS & CO., P. O. Box 63, Central City, Colorado.

JAMES A. LADD,

HOUSE AND SIGN PAINTER,

PAPER-HANGER AND CALCIMINER.

Residence on Casey Avenue. Orders left at Jno. Best's Pharmacy will receive prompt attention.

The Stalker & Standley property on the California consists of 600 feet. The main shaft is 700 feet deep. The surface ore of these claims produced about $50,000. An extensive pinch was then encountered, and after that had been passed, the mine produced from July 18, 1868, to July 18, 1870, $231,540 from mill gold alone. Receipts for smelting ore during this time would swell the amount to about $300,000 in two years, of which very nearly 50 per cent. was profit. The mill ore ran from $12 to $40 per ton in coin.

The Indiana and Hidden Treasure have also yielded well for the amount of work done, the ore running from five to eleven ounces per cord for one and a half years. There is little doubt that this whole vein, from one cause and another now idle, has produced three-quarters of a million of dollars. The

Mercer County and *Flack*—Covering more than 2,000 feet upon a parallel vein, is another noted property now idle. The Flack was once one of the main producers, the ore running as high as $700 per cord. The

Symond's-Forks—In 1862–'63, yielded nine ounces per cord, as an average yield of the ore run by 30 stamps. The

American Flag—Has produced not less than $200,000.

We might go on and mention the Corydon, Adeline, Wilbur, Whiting, and others in Central City district, the Harsh, Leavenworth, Woods, Topeka, Bench, Saratoga, Nottaway, Alps, and scores more in Russell district, and in every district more or less, but we must stop somewhere.

TELLER HOUSE,

W. H. BUSH, Proprietor,

Central City, - Colorado.

Opened in 1872; Is elegantly furnished; First-class in all respects, and has 150 rooms.

COLLINS'
Cake and Tart Cutter.

STATE AND WINDOW — RIGHTS FOR SALE.

Address COLLINS & CO., P. O. Box 63, Central City, Colorado.

SUBSCRIBE FOR and ADVERTISE IN

GOLDRICK'S "OLD RELIABLE"

Rocky Mountain Herald,

DENVER, - COLORADO.

$3 a year, mailed free of postage to any address, East or West.

TUNNELS.

The advantages of tunnel mining were recognized at an early day. Not less than nine tunnel locations were made in early times to pierce Quartz hill, only two of which have been prosecuted to any considerable length. Most of the early locations crossed the veins at such shallow depths that they were abandoned. The segregation of lodes into small properties, and high prices, operated to prevent the driving of deep tunnels of great length. Within a few years, greater interest in these enterprises has been manifested. The advantages are, first of all, the natural drainage of the water above the tunnel, and diminished pump service below the tunnel. This factor remains constant in all cases, even where the mine is worked by a shaft. There are other advantages that pertain to some localities, but not to all. There are several tunnels in construction or in use in this county worthy of particular mention. One of the latest enterprises of the kind, is the

BELDEN & TENNAL TUNNEL.

This corporation was organized under the laws of Colorado, in August, 1875, with a capital stock of $500,000, shares $5 and non-assessable. A part of the stock was sold in December last for a working capital of $12,000, of which less than $2,000 has been expended.

The mouth of the tunnel is in Chase gulch, about one mile above Black Hawk, and a half-mile from Central City, and its course is southwesterly, under-cutting Casto mountain. The grade from the depot, smelting works, and mills of Black Hawk, to the tunnel mouth, is an easy one, and the roads good. The company has located a mill site near the mouth of the tunnel. At this writing the tunnel has been driven 255 feet, and the work is being pushed as fast as three shifts of men can drive it.

THE LODE PROPERTY

of this company consists of 8,200 linear feet, located upon five seperate veins already cut and to be cut by the tunnel. The first vein is the *Ellery*, a blind lode not before discovered, cut by the tunnel 117 feet from the mouth, December 21, 1875. This vein has been located westerly as the *Ellery* and easterly as the *Furnald*, making 1,500 feet on each side of the tunnel. The *Ellery* has been drifted 85 feet from the tunnel, and has produced nearly 200 tons of ore, yielding about $21 per ton under stamps. The pay vein being 40 inches in width, the cost of mining is about $2 per ton.

The next known lode to be cut by the tunnel is the *Black Quartz*, upon which the company owns 1,600 feet. This is 235 feet from the tunnel mouth, (only 115 feet from present face,) and will be reached early in August. It will be cut 150 feet from the surface, but only 11 feet below the company's shaft on that property.

The next lode is *The Belden & Tennal*, situated 500 feet from the mouth, upon which the company owns 1,000 feet.

The fourth known lode is the *R. P. Ranney*, reached at a distance of 675 feet from the mouth, and cut at a depth of 300 feet. The company owns 1,000 feet on this lode, and has two shafts, one of them being 144 feet deep.

The *American River*, upon which the company owns 1,600 feet, completes the list of the property owned by the company. It is proposed to continue this tunnel beyond the company's property, for exploration, and to secure a revenue from tunnel royalty or trackage from other mines. When the tunnel reaches the *R. P. Ranney* lode, its course will be turned to run on that vein 400 feet westward, when it will again take a southwesterly course, cutting the *Louis Napoleon*, owned by Bond Bros.; also the *Casto* and *Winnebago*, at about 400 feet from the surface, and about 1,000 feet from the mouth of the tunnel. Continued southerly, passing under Eureka gulch to the Gunnell, it would cut that lode at an estimated depth of 500 feet, and numerous other lodes on the same hill. If carried 3,600 feet southward, or 6,500 feet from its mouth, it would undercut all the great lodes on Quartz hill at a depth of 800 to 900 feet. This is, of course, no small undertaking.

but not such a one, with our present prospects, as should excite our special wonder. When it is considered, that one lode discovered by the tunnel, since it was started, is able to pay all expenses of the tunnel, it may reasonably be expected to pay better as more lodes are reached.

The officers of the company are, president and managing agent, D. D. Belden, of Central City, and secretary, H. R. Foster, of Denver.

THE BOBTAIL TUNNEL.

The location of this tunnel is in the western part of Black Hawk, its mouth being upon the main street from Black Hawk to Central. It was commenced by an association in 1863, and was then driven 250 feet, when work was suspended for some years. The company was then reorganized, and the work placed in charge of Mr. A. N. Rogers, superintendent of the Bobtail Gold Mining Company. It was completed to the Bobtail lode in 1872, a distance of 1,150 feet from the mouth of the tunnel, and has been run upon that vein about 1,000 feet. It cuts the Bobtail at a depth of 500 feet from the surface. At a distance of 574 feet from the mouth, it cuts the Fisk lode at a depth of 275 feet. The Fisk lode was extensively worked through the tunnel, but is now worked from the surface. On the completion of the tunnel to the Bobtail, the hoisting machinery of the Consolidated Bobtail Company was transferred from the surface to the tunnel, where it has been in operation ever since. A more extended notice of these works will be found under a notice of the Bobtail lode.

This tunnel is 7x8 in size, and the country rock through which it was driven is unusually hard. The cost of the later work, including track, was $32 to $38 per foot.

Besides the very great advantage of cheaper drainage afforded by this tunnel, in this case there is the probable advantage of the cheaper handling of the ore. The expense of keeping up 500 feet of shaft, of hoisting all the ore 500 feet farther, and of hauling the same down steep hills a distance of one mile, is avoided by the use of the tunnel. But there are numerous drawbacks to the system that make it undesirable under ordinary circumstances, unless the tunnel cuts the vein at a greater depth than 500 feet.

THE GERMAN TUNNEL.

This tunnel enters the mountain south of Central City, opposite Turnverein Hall. It has now reached a distance of 406 feet, and is in progress. Five lodes have been cut in its course thus far, the last being the Bugher lode. The known lodes that it will reach within a few hundred feet more, are numerous. In comparatively easy ground, the cost thus far has been light, from $8 to $12 per foot.

The capital stock is $15,000, in shares of $500 each. The officers are, president, Alex. Carstens; secretary, S. I. Lorah; treasurer, F. Pflum; superintendent, Jacob C. Franks.

THE BUGLE TUNNEL.

This is an enterprise of great magnitude projected by Bela S. Buell, Esq., of Central City. It is located as follows: Commencing at a point on Gregory gulch about 500 feet above the Buell mine, its course is nearly south, under-cutting Mammoth hill, Russell gulch, and the divide between Russell gulch and South Clear Creek, making its southern terminus in Dump gulch, Clear Creek county. The whole distance is three miles 1,060 feet, of which about one mile is in Clear Creek county. The grade of the tunnel rises from each termini, meeting at a point under Russell gulch only 255 feet from the surface, where there is a shaft 100 feet deep. Twenty-seven well known and prominent lodes would be cut by this tunnel, besides numerous less prominent or wholly unknown ones. Starting from the Gregory gulch terminus, in a distance of 450 feet, it would pass four lodes and reach the Kip lode at a depth of 216 feet. The Mammoth lode would be reached at 1,120 feet, and at a depth of 528 feet. The summit of Missouri hill would be under-cut 558 feet deep. The bed of Russell gulch at a distance of 5,300 feet, 255 feet below surface; Saratoga lode 483 feet below surface; the divide between Willis and Elkhorn gulches 872 feet; the main divide 950 feet below surface; the Seaton and others of that belt of noted silver lodes, at depths varying from 600 to 700 feet.

So far Mr. Buell has constructed only about 100 feet of the tunnel, sufficient for the present to protect his rights. It is estimated that the cost of the tunnel will not exceed $400,000, and that with one-fourth of this capital provided for, the enterprise could take care of itself. Working from both ends with proper drilling machines, the tunnel should be completed within ten years. The Sutro tunnel, over four miles from the entrance to the Comstock, has been driven about 2¾ miles, with no expectation of a revenue until the great mine is reached. This proposed tunnel has no one great objective point, but is designed to cut at great depth a score or two of well known strong gold and silver lodes in its course. It is a feasible undertaking, and should be commenced at an early day.

LA CROSSE TUNNEL.

This is one of the tunnel locations of the earliest days. Its mouth is on Nevada gulch at the lower end of Nevadaville. It has been driven between 1,000 and 1,100 feet, and has cut the Kansas, Burroughs, Missouri, and other lodes, and requires only 150 to 200 feet more to reach the Illinois and Ingalls. The last 400 feet was driven under the management of Mr. John Scudder. A very large body of low grade ore was reached under the " Patch diggings " on Quartz hill, which no doubt would be available, with a water power mill at the tunnel mouth.

THE QUARTZ HILL TUNNEL.

This tunnel company, like the *German*, is purely a home concern. Organized in February, 1866, upon a capital stock of $50,000, in fifty shares of $1,000 each, the shares assessable, the stock was subscribed for by thirty-eight men, many of them laboring men, and men of small means. In the ten years the tunnel has been driven 925 feet at a cost of about $40,000. Ten lodes of various sizes and quality have been cut by it. A comparatively short distance will bring its face into the neighborhood of some of the largest and best lodes on Quartz hill. This tunnel is a standing example of what may be accomplished by perseverance under difficulties. The officers of the company are, president, Hy. Altvater; vice-president, Fred. Folster; secretary, H. J. Kruse; treasurer, Henry Kruse; superintendent, J. H. Lafranz; trustees, Elias Goldman, L. C. Rockwell, G. Steinle, and William Hambley. The

Prospector Tunnel—Is a tunnel on the vein, located on the south side of Chase gulch. It has been driven 160 feet and is in progress. The lode is 3½ feet wide, and carries galena and iron pyrites ore, which assays four ounces gold, and thirty-six ounces silver. The capital stock is $15,000, in shares of $1,000 each, owned in Black Hawk, and assessable. The officers are George Brubaker, president; George Gould, secretary; Ed. S. Blake, treasurer. The latest tunnel enterprise is that of the

Buckeye Mining and Tunneling Company.—Incorporated under Territorial laws in February, 1876. From their prospectus it appears that the company own and are operating Buckeye Tunnels Nos. 1 and 2, which are located to under-cut Phœnix and Buckeye mountains, lying north from the valley of the South Boulder, four miles west of Rollinsville. The location is due north eight miles from Central and four miles south of Caribou. These tunnels are projected to work the mines of Phœnix district, once so productive, but of late, neglected. The size of the tunnels between timbers, is 5½ wide by 6½ feet high. Tunnel No. 2 is now about 200 feet in length and progressing. One lode has been cut, eleven feet in width. No. 1 tunnel has been driven seventy feet. The company have also secured ample water power for reduction works near the tunnel, 160 acres of valley and timber land, houses, etc. The officers of the company are, president, A. M. Cassiday; secretary, W. S. Hinman; treasurer and superintendent, D. R. Cassiday.

Numerous other tunnel enterprises have been projected and commenced, (including one by an English company, from a point below Black Hawk to the Middle Park, a distance of twelve miles or more,) but none that seem likely to be immediately continued.

STAMP MILLS.

A tabular statement of the mills in operation in this county, originally prepared for this work, shows the following facts: Number of stamp mills in operation, 29; number of stamps, 810; weight of stamps from 350 to 700 ℔s., averaging 500 ℔s.; run by steam exclusively, 17; by water exclusively, 5; by both, 7; speed, from 25 to 32 drops per minute, averaging 30; fall of stamp in inches when shoe and die are new, 14 to 18 inches, averaging 15 inches; height of issue above die, given from 9 to $12\frac{1}{2}$ inches averaging $11\frac{1}{2}$ inches; the duty per stamp is given at one ton per 24 hours; wood consumed per ton, one-tenth of a cord; and when coal is used one-eighth to one-tenth of a ton. Wood is delivered at mills in Black Hawk for $5.50 per cord, and coal at same point at $5 per ton. Coal has taken the place of wood in numerous mills and mines, making the monthly consumption of coal for this purpose about 1,000 tons.

The changes in the construction of stamp mills, and the improvements in the methods of treatment within the last ten years, have been numerous and important in results, but not radical in character. Mortars are made "closer," with less waste room around and between the stamp heads. Mortar bottoms are made thicker, being five or six inches thick under the dies. Stamp heads are made eight inches in diameter. Tappets are generally movable on the stems (fastened by screw and key or other device,) but some of the best mill men prefer and use fixed tappets, effecting the necessary uniformity of drop by changing shoes and dies. Many solid cams are still used, but cams cast in halves are considered better on account of the convenience of replacing broken ones. The cams in use have a great variety of curvature. The involute is the curve adopted by Mr. Rogers in the new Bobtail mill, as being the only curve that answers all the required conditions. Iron guides to stamp stems have gone out of use, wooden guides being more cheaply made and quickly adjusted. Screens are of Russia iron, punched by machine, with seven or eight slots per square inch, the slots being about half an inch long and of the fineness of a sixty mesh seive. All the mills have single issue excepting the Briggs Bros'. 50-stamp mill. These successful and experienced mine operators, commend the double-issue mill as crushing more and amalgamating an equally high percentage, but the plan has not been generally adopted. The Kimber mill has Chilian mills at the foot of the tables, regrinding the pulp and passing it over other copper tables, with good results; on some ores amounting to $1 per ton with slight cost. Blanket sluices below the tables with pans for regrinding and amalgamating the blanket washings, are found in several mills, and several have small "miniature" pans for grinding the amalgam, a decided convenience in cleaning large lots. Tailings are generally buddled by hand, only one mechanical buddle—that in the Briggs mill—being now in use. The concentrated product is sold to the smelting works, and upon some ores makes no inconsiderable addition to the stamp mill product. The chemical chiefly used on the amalgamating coppers, is the cyanide of potassium, although aqua ammonia and other things are used under certain circumstances. The improvement in the care of coppers, is in the direction of using less chemicals than formerly, rather than more. Great care is taken to clean the whole surface of the copper, leaving no spots of hard amalgam. The improvements in the stamp mill and methods of operation, do not make much of a showing on paper, but such mechanical changes as have been made and the greater care observed, have increased the yield upon the same ore at least 25 per cent. To obtain the average yield of the mill ore as it comes from the small mines of the county, it was thought best to take the books of three custom mills, one in Nevada and two in Black Hawk; we therefore obtained from the mill books of the Whitcomb mill in Nevada, the S. & J. Mellor mill, Black Hawk, and of the Kimber mill, Black Hawk, the following results:

Mr. A. H. Tucker leased the Truman Whitcomb 25-stamp mill July 1, 1874, and it has been run solely on custom ore, mostly from Nevada and Illinois Central districts. The total amount of ore run to May 1, 1876, a period of 22 months, was 1,463 cords, or 10,241 tons of ore, yielding 10,071 ounces of retort gold, worth $15 per ounce, coin, equal to a product of $150,065 coin. Reckoning the currency value at $16.50 per ounce, the currency product was $166,171.50. This shows a yield of $14.66 in coin per ton, or $16.12 in currency. There were 565 separate and distinct lots of ore run, from nearly 100 lodes, and of course included many test lots of three, four or five tons each, which were found too lean for profitable mining.

The statement from the Kimber mill books covers a still longer period, from March 1, 1872, to January 1, 1876, three years and ten months. During the first fifteen months of this time, the mill had 32 stamps, and for the remainder of the time 35 stamps. This has been and still is a representative mill, and very popular with the miners. It is situated on North Clear Creek, one-quarter of a mile above the centre of Black Hawk. The construction of every part is the result of years of experience and careful study on the part of Mr. J. V. Kimber. As before mentioned, in addition to the stamp mill and amalgamating tables, there are eight Chilian mills of four feet diameter, with two rollers, each weighing 500 ℔s., and each receives the pulp from one battery, after passing over the usual copper surface. These mills discharge upon still other tables below. The power is furnished by a 40-horse power Woodbury engine during the winter months, and by an overshot water wheel of 23 feet diameter and 6 feet breast during five or six months in the summer. The mill site is 950 feet long and the fall 20 feet. The entire works are enclosed in a fire-proof stone building 95x65, which also gives the mill an even and moderate temperature during the coldest weather. During the period above-mentioned, there were about 60 separate lots of ore treated each month and the whole number of lodes represented is over 150. The computation shows that 3,880 cords or 27,160 tons yielded 16,942 ounces of retort gold, worth $15.50 per ounce, or $262,601, coin value, or an average yield of $9.67 per ton, coin, equal as an average of the whole time to $10.83 per ton, currency.

The Mellor mill statement covers the twelve months ending January 1, 1876. The ore worked at the mill was from a smaller number of lodes, and embraced some of the first-class as regular customers. During this time there were 5,040 tons of ore treated, producing $57,902.60, coin, a yield of $11.48 per ton, coin, or $12.63, currency, averaging gold through the year at $1.10.

Combining these statements, we find that 6,063 cords or 42,441 tons of ore from 200 different lodes, produced 30,632 ounces of bullion, worth $470,568, coin; an average yield of $11.09, coin, per ton, or $12.20, currency, per ton.

This is believed to be the most complete statement of mill yield ever given to the public, but it should not be understood as the average yield of Gilpin county mill ore. To compute that average exactly, is impossible. To arrive at an approximate estimate, the large masses of ore from the Buell and Briggs mines, upon which there is a fair margin when yielding $8 to $9 per ton, and the Ophir-Burroughs mill ore yielding $26 per ton, should both be considered.

BOSTON & COLORADO SMELTING WORKS.

The enterprise of the Boston & Colorado Smelting Company was inaugurated in the spring of 1867.

Prof. N. P. Hill spent the summers of 1864–'65 in Gilpin county, and thus became familiar with its mines, ores, etc. He visited Swansea, Wales, in the winter of 1865–'6, and returned to Colorado in the spring of 1866 accompanied by Mr. Hermann, of Vivian & Sons' Works, Swansea, and by Mr. Lewis, of the firm of Nayler & Co. Seventy tons of ore from the Trust mine, Bobtail lode, were purchased by Mr. Lewis from H. B. Brastow, and forwarded by cattle trains to Atchison, thence to Swansea by way of New Orleans.

Prof. Hill made his second visit to Swansea in the winter of 1866–'67, to witness the working of the ore, and soon after decided to engage in the smelting business in Colorado. About this time he resigned his professorship of chemistry in Brown University.

Returning in the spring of 1867, he organized a company in Boston, under the title of the Boston & Colorado Smelting Company, with a full paid capital of $275,000. He reached Colorado in June, 1867, and with Mr. H. Berger as superintendent of construction and of the smelting processes, and Mr. W. A. Abbe of Boston in charge of the work, commenced the erection of the establishment.

One smelting furnace and one calcining furnace, with the necessary crushing machinery, were completed in the fall of 1867. The first smelting was done in January, 1868. From that time to the present, there has never been a day when the works have not been in full operation. Since then three additional smelting furnaces have been added; one in 1869, one in 1871, and one in 1875. Seven calcining furnaces have also been added to the establishment, as follows : one in 1868, one in 1869, two in 1870, one in 1872, and two in 1874.

In 1873, a branch establishment was built at Alma, South Park, under the superintendence of H. R. Wolcott. It consists of two smelting furnaces, crushing machinery, etc. It has done a large and successful business, and has been entirely under the direction of Mr. Wolcott, (with Mr. Berger as metallurgist for the first year,) until January 1, 1875, when Mr. Wolcott was appointed assistant superintendent at Black Hawk, and Mr. H. Williams was put in charge at Alma.

Until the summer of 1873, the operations of the company were confined entirely to concentrating the ores into matte, containing gold, silver and copper. This product was sold to Vivian & Sons at Swansea, under a contract made before the works were built. At this time, Vivian & Sons terminated the contract by notice of a large reduction in price for the matte, a reduction so large as to make it impossible for the company to continue its business on the old plan without a corresponding reduction in the price of ore. The result of this movement was to force the company into the separating and refining business, which has added a most important branch of business to the industries of the county. The capital was increased to $500,000 by the payment of $225,000 into the treasury and since that time not less than $750,000 have been constantly employed in their business.

The company was fortunate in securing the services of Mr. Richard Pearce, who had an extensive experience in a similar business in Swansea. The refining works were put in full operation in October, 1873, the first shipment of silver bars being made about the first of November of that year. From that time until the first of June of the present year, about *eighty-one tons of pure silver* have been sent from these works.

The separation and refining of the gold, followed closely upon that of the silver. This was done at first by making a rich alloy of gold and copper, which was sent to the works of the company erected in Boston for the purpose. Here the gold was separated from the copper by the use of sulphuric acid, and a large quantity of sulphate of copper was manufactured. During the past year a great improvement in this process has been made by Mr. Pearce, and all the gold produced in the establishment is now sent direct to the mint in bars of a high state of fineness. The Boston works which were under the charge of Mr. N. F. Merrill, owing to this discovery, have been abandoned.

This important enterprise still remains in charge of Prof. N. P. Hill, general manager; H. R. Wolcott, assistant manager; R. Pearce superintendent of the processes, and A. von Schulz, assayer. The works cover a large tract of ground, and consist of eight groups of buildings. The store house for the richer ores, is a stone building 80x150 feet. Two crushing houses, each containing Blake crushers and Cornish rollers, have a capacity of 80 tons per day. The smelting house, containing four furnaces, is a building 50x160 feet. A line of buildings 75x250 feet is furnished with eight calcining furnaces each 40 feet long. The buildings for gold and silver refining, are 75x200 feet. They contain two calcining furnaces, two melting furnaces the fine grinding Bolthoff mill, a leaching room 50x100 feet, and melting and refining rooms for gold and silver. A separate brick building contains the furnaces for the reduction and refining of copper. These with office buildings, laboratories, shops, and barns, complete the list. In all there are seventeen furnaces. Over four acres of ground are well covered with buildings, stores of ore, etc. Fifty-two tons of ore are smelted daily. The items of fuel and labor require a daily outlay of $500.

The following general description of the processes is copied from the Denver *Mirror* of December 26th, 1875: "The low grade ores having been broken into lumps the size of hen's eggs, 75 to 100 tons in a heap are piled upon a square layer of wood, which being fired and consumed in about 12 hours, thoroughly ignites the mass which is covered with fine screened ore to make combustion less rapid and prevent melting. This roasting process continues two months until all the sulphur has been consumed that is contained in the sulphurites of copper and iron. Richer gold ores and those too fine to work in this way, are roasted in reverberatory furnaces. The ores (after roasting), are next taken to the smelting furnaces, the charges for which are made up of five or six different kinds of ore so combined that they flux each other, and produce the best possible results. This combination is determined in the laboratory, and requires the greatest skill and knowledge of ores. A reduction in the average time of smelting a charge of ore from 8 hours to 6, is equivalent to a saving of $75,000 per annum. No fluxes, properly speaking, such as lime, fluor spar or iron are used. In this process of smelting the ore is separated into a matte and slag—the amount of matte representing five per cent. of the original amount of ore smelted. This matte carries all the gold, silver and copper contained in the ore, every 20 tons of ore being concentrated into one ton of matte. After crushing, the matte is next treated by an ingenious process of roasting and leaching, and the silver extracted. The residue, after eliminating the silver, is again put into matte, (by smelting), and from this the gold is extracted by a process not in use by any other smelters in the world; in fact, being original with Mr. Richard Pearce. A full description of this process would require much space, with scarcely a chance of being intelligible to the general reader. The separation is performed without the use of acids or chemicals, the gold being taken directly from the gold matte by furnace processes. Silver amounting to a weekly production of $26,000, is sent to the New York mint, of an average fineness of 999, as shown us by the returns from that office. It undergoes no further refining, but is stamped as fine silver with a charge to the company of ¼ of of one cent per ounce."

The importance of this establishment to the leading interests of Colorado, may be estimated by the following statement of the value of bullion and matte produced, during the eight years it has been in operation, the figures for which have been taken from the books of the company, amounting to eight millions fifty-eight thousand one hundred and sixty-two dollars. We could wish for no better exponent of the constantly increasing prosperity of the mining business in our county and in the Territory, than the following statement of the yearly

PRODUCTION OF THE WORKS.

1868,	$ 270,886 00
1869,	489,875 00
1870,	652,329 00

1871,	848,571 00
1872,	999,954 00
1873,	1,210,670 00
1874,	1,638,877 00
1875,	1,947,000 00
Total,	$8,058,162 00

It is scarcely necessary to add to this exhibit, that this splendid success has been achieved through the untiring energy and great business ability of the managers on the one hand, coupled with the highest metallurgical skill upon the other.

COLLOM'S CONCENTRATION WORKS.

Mr. John Collom is the inventor of dressing machines, which have been for years successfully and almost exclusively used on the ores of the Lake Superior mines, and which have a large manufacture and sale in England. It was found that the character of Colorado ores, both gold and silver, required a differently constructed machine. After long and careful experiments, suitable machinery was devised and put in operation at Idaho Springs. In the summer of 1874, similar dressing works were put into the Keith or Mammoth mill on North Clear creek, in the upper part of Black Hawk. They were operated on Gilpin county ores for a few months, and closed for the lack of a satisfactory market for their concentrated product. Mr. Collom's company at once set about raising the necessary capital for building smelting works at Golden. Their furnaces are now nearly ready for work, and will have a capacity, when completed, of 32 tons per day. The concentration works at Black Hawk were reopened in March, and have since been in constant operation, treating about 62 tons of common stamp mill rock per day. The prices paid are almost uniformly larger than is netted by sending the same grade of ore to stamp mills, not infrequently reaching from two to three times as much. While there is a feeling, born of past sad experience, that this system may not prove the great advance that it seems, only the constitutionally conservative and those adversely interested, are without hope and faithless in its success.

Only a general description of these works can be attempted. The ore is crushed by a Blake crusher and two sets of Cornish rollers. Water is admitted with the ore to prevent clogging. The ore is then automatically sampled by Collom's patent sampler, a very simple but perfect device. The revolving screens separate the ore into eleven sizes, after which each size is conducted to its appropriate size of jigs, where the mineral is separated from the sand. The slimes are carried over to three pairs of revolving tables, and treated in three grades of fineness. The work done appears to be very perfect, so far as loss of value is concerned. The manager says, that with a few ores containing antimonial zinc blende, the tailings have contained as high as $3 per ton, but usually the loss in the tailings is not over 50 cents per ton. He denies that much, if any free gold, passes off with the tailings, and the loss, such as it is, is a laminated mineral of impalpable fineness. The usual proportion of concentrated material is as one to four or five of the original rock. The price list is based not only upon the assay, but upon the per cent. of mineral or pyritous material. Thus, for example, $20 ore with 20 per cent. of sulphides, is worth $7 per ton; but $20 ore with 10 per cent. of sulphides is worth 30 cents per ton more for every 1 per cent. less than 20 per cent., or $3 plus $7=$10, and $20 ore with 30 per cent. sulphides is worth only $4, or $7 less $3.

But for the failure of scores of other experimentors in this same line, and a consequent hesitation to believe that the apparent success is real and therefore permanent, no one would fail to recognize this as the greatest step in the progress of ore treatment in this county.

BOLTHOFF'S WET PULVERIZER.

This is the invention of Mr. Henry Bolthoff, of the firm of Hendrie Brothers & Bolthoff, foundrymen of Central City. It is a modification of the ball mill so successfully used for dry crushing, upon which Mr. Bolthoff has a valuable patent. This wet pulverizer consists of a cylinder 5 feet in diameter and 2½ feet in length, attached to a shaft making 24 to 30 revolutions per minute. The shell of the cylinder is of boiler iron, protected from wear on the inside by cast iron staves, together forming a corrugated surface. The cast iron cylinder-heads have grooves for the reception of the shell and the staves, leaving a recess between them through which the bolts pass from one head to the other. The cylinder-heads are protected on the inside by liners, which, like the staves, may be replaced when worn out. The ore, after being broken in a Dodge or Blake crusher, is fed in with water through one cylinder-head, by means of a nozzle tapering outward. Here it falls among 800 lbs. of cast iron balls, weighing from 6 to 12 lbs. each, which being carried up on the corrugated surface, are constantly falling and rolling towards the opposite side. When sufficiently pulverized to float, the pulverized material passes through the opposite cylinder-head, in which is a flaring copper lined nozzle. The thin pulp is then conducted to amalgamated copper tables, similar to stamp mill tables. Quicksilver is fed into the mill in small quantities from time to time, passes into the space between the staves and the shell, where it comes in contact with the pulverized ore which is passing back and forth between the staves. At 26 to 30 revolutions, its capacity, is equal to 15 stamps dropping 26 to 30 drops per minute, pulverizing equally fine. Run faster, its capacity is greater, and the tailings coarser. This mill costs only $1,000, requires only 10 or 12-horse power to drive it, is very compact, may be built so that it can be packed upon mules or jacks, and requires only such a foundation as will hold its weight, which is four tons. One of these mills was run for some months in the Bradley mill, Russell gulch, by Mr. L. E. Raldwin, but under such disadvantages as to furnish no satisfactory test of its merits in comparison with a stamp mill, either as a gold-saver or for economy of working. It has now been removed to Boulder county.

POWER DRILLS, AIR COMPRESSORS AND MAGNETIC BATTERIES.

The Burleigh drill and the Diamond drill were introduced and used in Clear Creek county some years since, but for some reason went out of use. In 1875, the Wood drill was introduced in the Caribou mine, Boulder county, and later in the White Cloud tunnel on North Boulder. In both of these cases the performance of the drill was entirely satisfactory. The Ingersoll drill has been introduced at the Sherman and No Name mines at Caribou, and gives satisfaction.

Within the past month or two, power drilling has been adopted in this county for the first time. Mr. A. N. Rogers, superintendent of the Consolidated Bobtail mine, has placed power drilling machinery in the tunnel level of that mine. It consists of a 45-horse power engine, driving an air-compressor of the Wood improved pattern, a horizontal, double-acting compressor, driven by crank connection with the engine, and making 80 strokes per minute. This size and speed of compressor will supply power for two such drills as are in use. The machines are of the Wood patent, and were put in operation by Mr. J. H. Van Vleet, the agent of the manufacturers. Those in use at the mine have a 3-inch piston, carry a drill 1⅛-inches diameter, have a cross bit, and bore 1½-inch hole. At present writing, they have been in operation but a short time, and have worked under some disadvantages, soon to be remedied, but have made the following results: First hole, 6 feet, in 20 minutes; subsequently, a drift worth $12 per foot by hand labor, was drifted 10 feet in 48 hours, three men handling the drill. The same level was driven 17 feet in six shifts of 10 hours, and 4 feet of heading has been made upon one shift. An average day's work for one drill is 50 feet of hole in 10 hours. Both drills are now in operation. When used in sinking the shaft, the comparative profit will be greater still. If the results with these two machines warrant it, a larger compressor or an additional one will be put in. Messrs. Hendrie Bros. & Bolthoff are the local agents for these drills.

Some months ago, Mr. Rogers purchased a Laflin & Rand magnetic battery, which he has used with satisfactory results. The object of exploding blasts with a battery, is to secure the simultaneous explosion of two or more shots, that each may " help " the others, and thus break more rock than if the shots were fired singly. The method of sinking a shaft by means of power drilling machines and magnetic exploders, is as follows: Suppose the bottom of a shaft, say 8x16, to be very nearly level. With the drilling machine two rows of holes are drilled across the breadth of the shaft—say three or four holes in each row—the two rows of holes pitching towards each other. The holes are then loaded with Giant, Hercules, Rendrock or any other of the nitro-glycerine compounds, the Laflin & Rand primers being first adjusted to the cartridge. These primers consist of a copper cylinder, $\frac{1}{4}$ of an inch in diameter, and $\frac{3}{8}$ long, closed at the top end, which is charged with fine saltpeter powder. Two small wires, each say 2 feet long, *nearly* meet inside the exploder, and are connected by a fine platinum wire, passing through the fine black powder. A percussion cap is adjusted to the lower end of the exploder, and imbedded in the cartridge. If common black powder is used for the charge, no cap is necessary. The exploder wires are then connected so as to form a circuit through all the charges, two insulated wires are now reeled off down the shaft from the first level above the bottom, and attached to the two unconnected ends of the exploder wires. The two insulated wires are now attached to the opposite poles of the battery, the crank of the battery is given a turn or two, generating a current of magnetic electricity sufficient to heat the fine platinum wire in the exploders to a degree that fires the fine powder, explodes the cap and charge in each hole at exactly the same instant. The rock removed, three or four more holes are drilled in each bench of ground, looking toward the water sump, before made by the double row of lifting shots, and these six or eight shots are fired in the same manner as before. It requires no great experience to see that the expense of sinking shafts, drifting or stoping, must be very largely reduced by these appliances. The cost of the battery mentioned, (on the principle of Farmer's battery,) is $180, and properly taken care of will last a life-time. The cost of exploders is the same as of fuse. Double-covered wire is furnished at two cents per foot.

PLACER MINING.

As has been said in another place, the larger part of the gulches were worked out in 1866. That part of Russell gulch lying between the mouths of Excelsior and Elkhorn gulches, has been worked every summer since with varying results, sometimes very good. This year, four companies will operate in that locality.

Creek mining has also been pursued every year on some part of North Clear creek, from its junction with the main creek to Black Hawk. The production of gold from this source was not large until since 1870, owing to the temporary character of the flumes put in. Every summer brought a flood, and consequent disaster, washing off the flume, gold and all, on a voyage to the Platte. Since 1870, the production has steadily increased.

The Cameron Mine.—This mine consists of 7,000 feet in length by 250 feet in width, of the bed of the creek. Work was commenced on this mine by Mr. Alex. Cameron in 1864, under a three years lease of 1,000 feet from W. B. Walling. The title to the whole 7,000 feet has been acquired from the proceeds of working. Very little was done in 1864. In 1865 and 1866, work was prosecuted vigorously and successfully, but in the latter part of 1866, a flood took out the flume and its contents. In the early part of 1867, high bed-rock was encountered, diminishing the yield. By July good ground was reached, and the mine paid $21 per day to the hand to the close of the season. Then came trouble with adverse claimants, vexatious and expensive law-suits, which were not settled until the fall of 1868. The mine continued good through the season of 1869, enabling Mr. Cameron to acquire title to the whole 7,000 feet since owned by him. During the summer of 1870, the average yield per man was $11 per day. (The writer verified this at the close of that season from bank certificates and time books.) In 1871, another high bed-rock had to be cut through, and the production was less. In '72, the production was $10 per day to the hand. In '73–'74, the mine was operated by "Chinese cheap labor," but it proved very dear labor. Mr. Cameron has a very poor opinion of Celestial mining. In 1875 it was leased to the Chinamen, they paying one-fourth of the gross proceeds. The result was a small dividend, but not half of what it would have been with regular miners.

The prospects for the future are very flattering. The flume is a very substantial one, having withstood the severest flood ever known on the creek. There remains about 5,000 feet of ground that has never been washed. The flume has just passed a high bed-rock, and will shortly be in first rate ground.

Since writing the above, we learn that this mine has passed into the hands of a stock company, with a capital of $100,000, shares $10 each. The trustees are Alex. Cameron, Lorenzo M. Freas, Thomas Mullen, Morris Thomas, and E. W. Cobb. The stock will be placed on the Colorado Stock Board.

From the Cameron mine to the mouth of Russell, the ground is nearly all worked out.

Next below, Messrs. Hugle & Hall have 2,000 feet of ground systematically opened, that pays from $3 to $15 per man. Then comes the Nelson or Pitman mine of 2,500 feet, about half worked out. This mine, since properly worked, has paid from $6 to $8 per man. Passing over a half mile of ground worked out ten years ago, we come to Freas' claim of 1,200 feet, now owned by Joseph Welch. One side has been worked out, and the other side has been yielding from $5 to $8 per day to the hand.

There are five other mines between the last mentioned and the forks of the creek, all of which have ground that will pay if properly worked, some of them paying every season.

MINERALS.

The following list of the principal minerals observed in Gilpin county, is kindly furnished us by PROF. J. ALDEN SMITH, who, as a mineralogist, is universally conceded to have no peer in the State. In recognition of his merits, the Legislative Council has thrice confirmed his appointment as Territorial Geologist. For many years he has been an examiner of mines, and in no instance has the practical result reversed his judgment. Parties wishing to sell " wild cat " property, will not find it to their advantage to secure his report. Parties buying may venture to be enthusiastic if his report is commendatory. As an expert examiner of either mines or minerals, he is a thoroughly informed, painstaking, conscientious and safe, adviser and judge. His early appreciation of the American mine at Sunshine, Boulder county, and his successful management of it to the present time, is one of many examples that might be given, in justification of our high opinion. Professor Smith says :

" THE COUNTRY ROCK,

or general formation is granitic, passing from a highly foliated mica schist, through gneiss, and gneissic granite to a true granite, generally of a very coarse structure. It is traversed by numerous dykes of porphyry, having a general northeast and southwest trend, approximately. Most of the valuable mines are in the granite, comparatively few valuable ore deposits having been found in the gneiss, and still less in the mica schist. The principal minerals thus far observed, are alphabetically arranged in the following

CATALOGUE.

Actinolite, Albite, Allophane, Amethyst, (some exceedingly fine specimens of this beautiful gem have been found at Nevada. One in the possession of the writer, 7x10 lines, is pronounced by lapidaries and jewelers to be the finest amethyst ever found in America.) Antimony, (sulphide, with copper and lead,) Arsenic, (sulphide, with iron and copper,) Bismuth, (native, carbonate, sulphide, oxyd and telluric,) Baryta, (sulphate,) Beryl, Calc Spar, Chalcedony, Chlorite. Crysolite, Copper, (native, pyrites, chalcopyrite, erubescite, tetrahedrite, tenorite, tennantite, cuprite, glance, malachite, chrysocolla, azurite, velvet ore,) Egeran, Epidote, (fine xls.,) Feldspar, (fine xls. of the sanidin variety abundant,) Garnets, Gold, (crystalized, massive, and in wires,) Graphic Granite. Hornblende, Iron, (bi-sulphuret, magnetic sulphuret, arsenical sulphuret, carbonate, sulphate, magnetic oxyd, hæmatites and ochres,) Lead, (sulphide, oxyd, carbonate, sulphate, phosphate, selenid and molybdate,) Manganese, (per oxyd and bin oxyd,) Meerschaum, Mica, Molybdenite, Opal, Porphyry, Quartz, (fine xls. and nearly all the massive varieties,) Silver, (native, glance, ruby, chlorid,) Sulphur, Talc, Tourmaline (black and brown,) Uranium, (oxyd, carbonate and sulphate,) Zinc, (sulphide, carbonate and silicate.)"

BULLION.

In the absence of any reliable data of the gold and silver shipments previous to 1870, it is simply impossible to give an unquestionable statement upon the production of Colorado or of Gilpin county. The writer has, however, devoted considerable time to an endeavor to give approximate results, admitting without argument that they may be too high or too low. Hollister in his *Mines of Colorado*, estimates the total product to June 30, 1866, at over $37,000,000. Commissioner Raymond believes that $30,000,000 would come nearer the truth. But for reasons satisfactory to the writer, this estimate is considered too high, and we estimate the production to the end of 1869, at $32,000,000

For 1870,	3,675,000
" 1871,	4,663,000
" 1872,	4,661,465
" 1873,	4,020,263
" 1874,	5,362,283
" 1875,	6,059,000
Total,	$60,441,011

Of which about $10,000,000 was silver and the balance gold.

The production of gold and silver from Gilpin county is as follows:

To January 1, 1870, (estimated,)	$25,000,000
For 1870,	1,267.900
" 1871,	1,378.100
" 1872,	1,389,289
" 1873,	1,440,502
" 1874,	1,695,804
" 1875,	2,010,391
Total for Gilpin county,	$34,181,986

The currency values of the stamp mill bullion for the first half of the current year, are compared below with those of corresponding months of last year.

	1875.	1876.
January,	$ 99,933 33	$ 99,232 40
February,	72,868 30	100,578 18
March,	87,610 05	144,300 22
April,	90,734 97	118,170 00
May,	85,097 51	113,550 00
June,	110,667 78	130,160 00
Total,	$546,911 94	$705,990 80

CENTRAL CITY LAND DISTRICT.

This land district was established in 1868. The whole number of applications for mineral entries to May 5, 1876, is 1,059. The whole number of mineral entries is 743, leaving 316 either in suspense, or waiting the expiration of publication notice. The number of mineral entries of Gilpin county property is 265, upon 178 different lodes, covering 211,578 linear feet, or over 40 miles of lode property.

The whole number of mineral patents issued in the United States is about 1,600, of which nearly one-third have been issued in this district. The following is a list of

MINERAL PATENTS ISSUED IN GILPIN COUNTY.

Name of lode.	District.	Linear feet.
Adaline,	Nevada,	200
Alma,	"	200
Arctic,	Lake,	1,400
Briggs,	Gregory,	800
Baxter & Crispin,	Central City,	1,600
Big Thunder,	Illinois Central,	1,600
Bates, (3 patents,)	Gregory,	762
Bobtail, (6 patents,)	"	632
Burroughs, (3 patents,)	Nevada,	584
Beacon of the West.	Russell,	1,400
Baker,	Nevada,	142
Billings, (2 patents,)	Gregory,	1,600
Bell,	Illinois Central,	1,400
Buckeye,	Nevada,	1,000
Bueno,	Gregory,	1,500
Columbia,	Nevada,	1,000
Corydon,	"	900
Camp Grove,	"	340
Coaley,	Enterprise,	1,500
Cook,	Gregory,	800

Name of lode.	District.	Linear feet.
Cork,	Nevada,	600
Confidence,	Illinois Central,	1,400
Cymso,	Nevada,	400
Continental,	Illinois Central,	500
Conjunction,	Russell,	3,000
Compensation,	"	"
Camper,	"	"
Circassian,	Mountain House,	1,400
Champion,	Eureka,	1,000
Champion,	Enterprise,	3,000
Calhoun, (2 patents,)	Russell,	650
Douglass,	Nevada,	900
Ellieth,	Gregory,	500
East Boston,	Central City,	1,600
Elliott,	Gregory,	500
Extenuate,	Illinois Central,	1,700
Epizootic.	Gregory,	1,500
Egyptian,	Illinois Central,	600
Flack,	Nevada,	295
Federal,	Russell,	1,600
Fisk, (9 patents,)	Gregory,	1,140
French, (2 patents,)	Russell,	2,300
Granite,	Gregory,	700
Gregory Extension,	"	300
Gardner, (4 patents,)	Illinois Central,	954
Gibson,	"	300
Gunnell,	Eureka,	454
Gilpin County,	Enterprise,	3,000
Grand River,	Nevada,	600
Golden Flint,	Independent,	1,400
Grisley,	Russell,	1,600
Grand Army,	Eureka,	1,600
Gregory, (4 patents,)	Gregory,	1,100
German,	"	2,000
Gregory No. 2,	Greg'y and Central City,	1,000
Hydrant,	Eureka,	800
Helena,	Russell,	3,000
Humboldt,	Gregory,	500

Name of lode.	District.	Linear feet.
Harsh,	Russell,	800
Hunter,	Gregory,	300
Heles	Nevada,	3,000
Hope No. 2,	Gregory,	1,500
Indiana,	Nevada,	200
Ingalls,	Illinois Central	800
Irving,	Nevada,	400
Ivanhoe,	"	2,100
Indian.	"	100
Illinois,	Illinois Central,	1,000
Justice,	Russell,	900
John Jay,	Eureka,	200
Jones & Matteson, 4 patents,)	Nevada,	1,100
Kansas, (10 patents,)	"	2,539
Kip,	Gregory,	1,200
Kent County.	Nevada,	900
Kokomo,	Russell,	3,000
Keystone,	Nevada,	700
Kirk,	Illinois Central,	1,500
Keystone,	Russell,	200
Louisiana,	"	1,500
Lyman,	Nevada,	500
Leavitt,	Gregory,	1,000
Lamberson & Warren,	Nevada,	1,600
Minnesota,	Russell,	1,400
Mat France,	Central City,	1,600
Mountain City,	Gregory,	1,100
Mountain,	Enterprise,	500
Mammoth,	Gregory and Enterprise,	3,846⅓
Michigan City Tunnel,	Gregory,	600
Motto,	Nevada	200
Mackie.	Illinois Central,	800
Martin,	Russell,	3,000
Missouri, (2 patents,)	Nevada)	950
Monroe, (2 patents,)	"	833
Mineral,	"	900
McCallister	Gregory,	1,500
Mercer County,	Nevada,	300

Name of lode.	District.	Linear feet.
National Bank,	Eureka,	1,400
Nottaway,	Lake,	700
Old Bullion,	Gregory,	1,000
Ohio,	Russell,	1,000
Peck & Thomas,	Gregory,	600
Pierce,	Central City,	400
Pozo,	Nevada,	1,400
Pewabic, (3 patents,)	Russell,	2,100
Pike's Peak,	Illinois Central.	600
Running,	Gregory,	900
Roderick Dhu,	Illinois Central,	500
Rocky Mountain Terror,	Russell,	1,400
Radical,	Enterprise,	1,500
R. P. Ranney,	Quartz Valley,	500
Symond's Fork,	Nevada,	630
Sapphire,	Eureka,	1,100
Sullivan,	Nevada.	250
Silver Cloud,	Enterprize,	1,600
Shaft,	Nevada,	3,000
Shaw,	Illinois Central,	1,100
Saint Louis,	Eureka,	300
Star of the West,	Lake,	2,600
Salopian,	Nevada,	700
Suderberg, (2 patents,)	"	1,400
Saratoga, (2 patents,)	Russell,	700
Shaffer,	Nevada,	100
Star of the West,	Russell	1,600
Searle,	"	2,000
Sugar Tit,	Nevada,	1,200
Slaughter House,	"	1,600
Tierney,	Gregory,	1,300
Topeka, (2 patents,)	Russell	400
Tigress,	Illinois Central,	400
Vanderbilt,	Nevada,	800
Vasa,	Gregory,	600
Wabash,	Enterprise,	1,400
Whiting,	Eureka,	1,900
Winslow,	Illinois Central,	1,000
West Pewabic,	Russell	3,000

CENTRAL CITY.

This principal town and county seat, is the mining and commercial centre, and has a population of about 3,000. It is flanked on the east by Black Hawk, and on the west by Nevada, forming a continuous settlement over three miles in length. Built upon Gregory gulch, and its branches, Eureka, Spring, and Nevada gulches, it was formerly an unsightly place, and can never cease to be " queer looking " to strangers. The fire of May 21, 1874, destroyed nearly all of the business houses of the city. sparing of the more prominent only the Teller House, the Register Block, and four stores. What seemed a calamity, was really a benefit. It opened an opportunity to widen, straighten and grade the streets; to establish fire limits, and to build better structures, without danger from adjoining old rookeries, all of which were speedily improved. In a little more than a year, nearly all the burnt district was occupied by substantial business blocks, many of them being in good city style.

Central—and Black Hawk also—has two daily mails to Denver, a daily stage, mail and express to Georgetown *via* Idaho Springs, and the same to Caribou *via* Nederland. The Western Union Telegraph lines extend to Caribou, Nederland, Boulder, Idaho Springs and Georgetown, as well as to Golden and Denver.

There are three banks, two national and one private. The Rocky Mountain National is the successor of Kountze Bros. of New York, Omaha, and Denver, by whom it is controlled. The First National is the successor of Thatcher, Standley & Co., who were the successors of Warren Hussey & Co. The banking house of Hanington & Mellor commenced business in 1875. Each of these enjoys and justly merits the public confidence.

The public school is an object of just pride. The granite school building was erected in 1870, at a cost of $25,000, and supplied with all the modern conveniences for teaching. The school is under the charge of a principal and four assistants, having an attendance of 315 scholars.

The St. Aloysius Academy, a parochial school under the management of the Roman Catholic denomination, was completed in 1875, at a cost of $16,000. It furnishes instruction to 100 pupils, including instruction in the French and German languages.

The Daily and Weekly *Central City Register*, established in 1862, is now the only newspaper in the county, having survived numerous competitors.

There are six church organizations in Central, each maintaining religious services in its own house of worship, viz : the Baptist, the Congregationalist, the Episcopal, the Methodist Episcopal, the Presbyterian and the Catholic.

The valuation of the city by the assessment of 1875, was $924,231, or about 42 per cent. of that of the county.

The fire department, since 1874, has been both efficient and enthusiastic. The water works of the city for fire purposes only, although limited as yet, cover the larger part of the business houses. The domestic supply, owing to the scarcity of good wells, is unique. The peripatetic water vendor, and owner of some fine springs in the upper part of the city, goes around with an iron tank holding ten barrels, and through a hose leading from tank to kitchen, pumps up or discharges downward, as the case may be, a barrel or two at the tune of *thirty-five cents per barrel!* What looks like a lack of public spirit in this matter is really something else. It would, however, require a larger book than this to elucidate the "Water Question" of Central City and Gilpin county. With an abundant supply for all purposes—milling, domestic and fire—within fourteen miles, private greed will not long be allowed to stand in the way of public interest.

The charter of the city of Central dates from 1864. The list of the present city officers will be found in the Official Directory.

BLACK HAWK.

This is the second town in size in the county, containing about 1,500 inhabitants. It is built along North Clear creek.

and upon two tributaries, Chase and Gregory gulches. The assessed valuation is $629,000. It adjoins Central City on its west line, apparently forming one town. It is the terminus of the Colorado Central railroad, and enjoys a good local trade. Within its limits are the Boston & Colorado Smelting Works, Collom's Concentration Works, some 16 stamp mills having 475 stamps in operation, together comprizing the principal reduction works of the county. It has one foundry and machine shop, boiler works, and one sampling mill. The public school building is a commodious one, costing $15,000, and the school, with an average attendance of 143, is divided into three grades, under the care of accomplished teachers. The Methodists and Presbyterians have each church edifices, in which they maintain public worship.

The city charter was approved March 11, 1864, the first city election held April 5, and the first meeting of the Council held April 12th of the same year.

NEVADAVILLE.

A mining town lying southwest of and adjoining Central City. To avoid confusion of names, the name of the post office at this place was changed to Bald Mountain. The town has a population of about 1,000, to whom employment is furnished by the large number of valuable mines in the near vicinity. The various mines on the Kansas, Burroughs, Missouri, Gardner, Rising Sun, Mercer County, California, Flack, Camp Grove, Indiana, American Flag, Hubert, Jones, Prize, Dyke, Suderberg, and scores more, are all within a quarter of a mile of the centre of the town. About 175 stamps are in operation, and more than this number are idle for want of a supply of water. When a full supply of water is brought into the county, as no doubt there will be at some future time, Nevada will become a great reducing as well as mining centre.

The town was incorporated July 7, 1870. A good public school is maintained in a school building that cost $3,000. The average attendance is 55. Commercial business is rather limited. There are two churches, Episcopal and Methodist Episcopal, both having houses of worship.

A FEW WORDS TO TOURISTS.

The visitor after a ride through the magnificent canyon of Clear Creek by the Colorado Central railroad, and especially after a stage ride from Georgetown or Caribou, has a keen appetite, induced by that best of all tonics, mountain air. His first question is, "Where shall I stop?" Well, the Teller House, a 150-room hotel at Central, is *the* hotel of the county.

"What is there to see?" If you are interested in the various processes by which the ores are mined and the gold and silver extracted from the ore, take a 'bus or carriage and visit the mines, mills and works on the main thoroughfare to and in Black Hawk. Call at Buell's mine and mill on the Leavitt lode; then at Briggs' mine and mill, and go up and see the Gregory mine-pump; then you want to go and see the Bobtail tunnel, (Mr. Rogers is very good-natured,) and see the machinery and what a mine looks like. If you want to see one of the largest and best stamp mills, call at the Bobtail mill, Black Hawk. Then turn up North Clear Creek and see Collom's Concentration Works. It is worth anybody's while to see how perfectly that machinery separates the mineral from the sands. Then drive down to the Boston & Colorado Smelting Works. Messrs. Hill, Pearce and Wolcott, are very very polite to strangers; but do not dream of getting more information than this book affords. You will see heaps of raw ore, roasted ore, molten ore, slag, matte, silver in solution clear as crystal, silver in deposition, silver in drying tanks, and pure silver in bricks; gold and copper in process, and the former in bars and the latter in ingots, both nearly pure. Then back to dinner and rest. This is enough for one day. Do not attempt too much. The mountain air is as exhilerating to strangers as champagne, stimulating to over-exertion. Hasten rather slowly, especially up hill. If one has time and inclination to look into the business further, there are plenty of tunnels, mines and mills in all directions. Our manufacturing establishments are limited to breweries and foundries.

THE SCENERY.

There are three views easily accessible from Central, of conceded beauty and grandeur. Bald Mountain, 1¼ miles from Central, presents a very beautiful view in all directions. It is about 9,000 feet in height, or 1,000 feet above Central. The summit is easily reached on horseback, and nearly reached by carriage. Belleview Mountain, 2½ miles distant, lying west of Virginia canyon on the Idaho road is another much admired locality. Many noted travelers in this country have said that no other view in the mountains exceeds this in beauty. Both of these mountains may be visited in a half day's drive.

A trip to James' Peak, one of the peaks of the great Rocky Mountain range, 10 miles distant, should by no means be omitted. If the trip is made on horseback, one may ride nearly to the summit. If by carriage, there is a half mile of easy mountain climbing. This peak is 13,200 feet in height and overlooks the Middle Park on the west, the range north and south from Long's Peak to Gray's Peak, and eastward the view covers 35 miles of mountains falling off towards the plains, the Platte valley, and the high divide and table lands for 75 miles east and southeast of Denver. With a glass, Denver and the railroad trains passing in and out, are easily discerned. This peak is the most accessible of all the peaks of the great chain, the view is equal to that on any of the peaks, and has the advantage of being usually free from clouds. No other view in the mountains pays so well for the cost and trouble of seeing it. An early morning ride to the peak, the climb, the views, the return to camp, the picnic by the mountain brook, the return ride in the evening shadows, make up a day of keen enjoyment to the least romantic. There are other peaks of the range higher than James', but so frequently are their summits shrouded in mist or surrounded with an impenetrable haze, that the toilsome two day's trip is a sore disappointment. As an

OUTFITTING POINT

for a trip to the Middle Park, Central City has no superior. Everything needed for such an excursion, can be obtained there at reasonable prices. There are

THREE ROUTES TO THE PARK.

The shortest is the James' Peak wagon road and trail beyond. Central to James' Peak, 10 miles; from the Peak to Cozens' Ranch, 12; Cozens' to Junction, 6; Junction to Carpenter's, 4. Here the road forks, one road leading to Grand Lake, 30 miles distant, and the other to Hot Sulphur Springs, 12 miles distant, making the distance from Central to the springs only 44 miles, which has several times been traveled in a day. But there are good camps and stopping places, if the ride is too much for one day.

The route by the Berthoud Pass wagon road, is only 10 miles longer from Central than from Georgetown. The distances are as follows: Central to Fall River House, 7; thence to Empire, 8; thence to Cozens', 18; thence to Junction, 6; thence to Carpenter's, 4; thence to Hot Sulphur Springs, 12; total, 55 miles. Parties taking public conveyance go by way of Georgetown. At Empire, Cozens', Carpenter's and the Springs, will be found hotel accommodations and stabling for animals.

The third route is by the Rollinsville and Middle Park wagon road *via* the Boulder Pass. Rollinsville is on the Caribou road 12 miles from Central, and twenty miles from Boulder. The distance from Rollinsville to Hot Sulphur Springs is 40 miles; to Grand Lake, 35; to Campbell & Baker's mines, 45; to Egeira Park, 65; to Gore Range, 75; to Bear River, 120; to Elk Mountain mines, 150 miles. One day's drive will bring the traveler into the park, 20 miles from Rollinsville. There are good camping places on both sides of the range. About 6 miles travel may be saved by taking the Pine Creek road *via* Newell's saw-mill, reaching the Rollinsville and Middle Park road 6 miles from Rollinsville, making the distance from Central to Hot Springs only 46 miles. Both the Berthoud Pass and Rollinsville and Middle Park roads are toll-roads.

COLORADO CENTRAL RAILROAD.

The scenery on the line of the Colorado Central, mountain division, is not excelled by that of any other line of travel. The road is narrow-gauge—3 feet—as indeed it must be, to successfully run the curves foreordained by nature on this line. Like Hudibras' politician, it "wires in and wires out," but one is never in doubt whether he is coming in or going out, on a grade of 200 feet to the mile. Neither pen pictures or photographs do justice to the scenery, but a dozen or two views by Jos. Collier, of Central, will be among the tourists most cherished souvenirs of a trip through Clear Creek canyon.

BUSINESS.

From a table prepared for the *Register* by Mr. Nagle, agent of the Colorado Central at Black Hawk, we condense the following statement of freight receipts at Black Hawk during the year 1875:

	Tons.
Ore,	3,704.06
General merchandise,	5,972.12
Coal,	5,981.71
Hay,	1,956.41
Corn,	639.30
Oats,	530.63
Flour.	787-14
Mill Stuff,	542.93
Total,	20,114.30

The coal traffic steadily increased throughout the year, from 242 tons in January to 863 tons in December. In January of this year, the coal receipts were 991 tons; February 973 tons, and in March, 1,175 tons.

SOCIETIES—CENTRAL CITY.

Central City Lodge No. 6, A. F. & A. M.—Frank C. Young, W. M.; Richard C. Lake, S. W.; David C. Collier, J. W.; Oscar Lewis, Treas.; Samuel I. Lorah, Secretary. Regular meetings second and fourth Wednesdays of each month.

Central City Chapter No. 1, R. A. M.—Ben. W. Wisebart, M. E. H. P.; Richard C. Lake, K.; Thomas H. Potter, Treas.; Samuel I. Lorah, Secretary. Regular meetings second and fourth Mondays in each month.

Central City Council No. 54, R. & S. M.—Foster Nichols, T. I. G. M.; Frank C. Young, D. G. M.; Ben. W. Wisebart, Treas.; Samuel I. Lorah, Recorder. Regular meetings third Wednesday of each month.

Central City Commandery No. 2, K. T.—Henry M. Teller, E. C.; Harper M. Orahood, Gen'lo; William Fullerton, Capt. Gen'l; Benj. T. Wells, Treas.; Samuel I. Lorah, Recorder. Regular meetings third Thursday of each month.

Rocky Mountain Lodge No. 2, I. O. O. F,—Stephen T. Hale, N. G.; John Cox, V. G.; Samuel Robins, Secretary; Thomas Williams, Treas.; Alonzo Furnald, D. D. G. M. Regular meeting every Thursday of each week.

Rising Star Lodge No 20, I. O. O. F.—John B. Hinman, N. G.; Henry Dorris, V. G.; L. Alexander, Secretary. Regular meeting every Friday evening.

Colorado Encampment No. 1, I. O. O. F.—Thomas Hambley, C. P.; Samuel Walters, H. P.; Samuel Rule, S. W.; Henry Dorris, Scribe; Joseph Haubrich, Treas. Regular meetings first and third Monday evenings in each month.

Gilpin Lodge No. 5, K. of P.—Chancellor Commander, Thos. Hambley; Vice Chancellor, Wm. Mitchell; Keeper of Records and Seal, Ed. Tippett; Master of Finances, L. Alexander; Master of Exchequer, George B. Bernstein, Regular meetings every Wednesday evening.

Central City Lodge No. 1, *I. O. G. T.*—Rev. L. J. Hall, W. C. T.; Mrs. M. H. Root, W. V. T.; Caleb Hale, Secretary; John Bettens, Treasurer. Regular meeting every Tuesday evening.

Carroll Encampment No. 2, *I. C. R. C.*—Roger F. Power, E. C.; James Davidson, Em. Coun.; Wm. Woodruff, S. C.; Mrs. Erena Parker, Rec. Sec'y; Miss May Putnam, Treasurer. Regular meetings every Friday evening.

Miners and Mechanics' Association.—President, John Cox: Vice-President, John Robins; Treasurer, William Bennetts; Secretary, Warren Dunstan. Regular meetings last Saturday in each month.

Warren Camp No. 2, *Knights of the New World.*—Worthy Chief, John Elrod; Assistant Chief, Joseph Ernst; Chaplain, Hugh Bailey; Recording Scribe, John H. J. Kruse; Financial Secretary, E. Traupel; Treasurer, Claus Schlapkohl. Regular meetings every Monday evening.

Rocky Mountain Turnverein.—First Speaker, Chris. Urick; Second Speaker, Barnabas Huber; Treasurer, H. J. Kruse; Recording Secretary, B. H. Koch; Corresponding Secretary, G. Wohlgesinger; First Turnward, George Borstadt; Second Turnward, Joseph Ernst. Regular meetings third and fourth Sundays of each month.

Rescue Hose Company No 1.—Foreman, N. H. McCall; First Assistant, Robert A. Campbell; Second Assistant, Silas R. Teats; Secretary, E. A. Whiting; Treasurer, E. H. Lindsey.

Rough & Ready Hook and Ladder Company No 1.—Foreman, A. A. McFarlane; First Assistant, J. A. Ladd; Second Assistant, J. M. Peterson, Recording Secretary, B. H. Koch; Financial Secretary, John B. Collins; Treasurer, Samuel V. Newell.

BLACK HAWK.

Black Hawk Lodge No. 11, *A. F. & A. M.*—John B. Ballard, W. M.; John S. Boylan, S. W.; Richard W. Mosley, J. W.; Alonzo Smith, Treasurer; Fred. A. Rudolph, Secretary. Regular meetings second and fourth Thursdays in each month.

Colorado Lodge No. 3, *I, O. O. F.*—R. Batchelder, N. G.; P. B. Wright, V. G.; Wm. Otterbach, Treasurer; Fred. A. Rudolph, Secretary. Regular meetings every Tuesday evening.

Harmony Encampment No. 11, *I. O. O. F.*—Wm. Otterbach, C. P.; Samuel H. Bradley, H. P.; G. B. Holstein, Treasurer; Fred. A. Rudolph, Secretary. Regular meetings first and third Friday evenings in each month.

Black Hawk Lodge No. 4, *K. of P.*—Chancellor Commander, George Fairbairn; Vice Chancellor, Samuel Haubrich; K. of R. and S., Fred French; Master of Finance, Otto Sauer; Master of Exchequer, Samuel Pelton. Regular meetings every Wednesday evening.

Excelsior Encampment No. 7, *I. C R. C.*—E. C., Benjamin Hensley; Em. Coun., Edw'd Dunstan; S. C., Frank Hill; Treasurer, Wm. Fick; C. of H., Geo. M. Freeman. Regular meetings every Thursday evening.

Scandia Society.—President, Oscar Scott; Treasurer, John Johnson; Secretary, Oscar Sodequist. Regular meetings every Saturday evening.

NEVADAVILLE.

Nevada Lodge No. 4, *A. F. & A. M.*—W. M. Finley, W. M.; W. J. Lewis, S. W.; P. A. Kline, J. W.; J. A. Shanstrom, Treasurer; J. W. Ratliff, Secretary. Regular meetings second and fourth Saturday evenings in each month.

Nevada Lodge No. 6, *I. O. O. F.*—Joseph Kline, N. G.; Wm. Richards, V. G.; John Hancock, Treasurer; James Morrish, Secretary. Regular meeting every Wednesday evening.

Bald Mountain Encampment No 3, *I. O. O. F.*—John Cox, C. P.; M. Moore, H. P.; John Sowell, Treasurer; James Morrish, Scribe. Regular meetings second and fourth Tuesday evenings in each month.

Nevada Lodge No. 3, *I. O. G. T.*—W. C. T., James Lawry; W. V. T., Mrs. John W. Ratliff; W. R. S., Thos. V. Lawry; W. T., Mrs. Jane Rowe. Regular meetings every Friday evening.

OFFICIAL DIRECTORY—1876.

UNITED STATES OFFICERS.

Second Judicial District.—Associate Justice, Jas. W. Stone; Clerk of District Court, Chase Withrow.

Land Office.—Register, Joseph M. Marshall; Receiver, Edward W. Henderson.

United States Commissioner.—James Burrell, Central.

Deputy United States Marshal.—C. P. Hoyt, Golden.

Postmasters.—Central, Eben Smith; Black Hawk, Elam C. Beach; Bald Mountain, (Nevadaville,) John W. Ratliff; Rollinsville, Fred. Gooch.

GILPIN COUNTY.

Commissioners.—Foster Nichols, (chairman,) James Clark, Job. V. Kimber.

Clerk and Recorder.—Joseph W. Bostwick.

Treasurer.—Bernhard H. Koch.

Sheriff.—William J. Buffington.

Surveyor.—Hal Sayr.

Coroner.—Robert G. Aduddell.

CENTRAL CITY—MUNICIPAL.

Mayor.—Benjamin W. Wisebart.

Treasurer.—Robert A. Campbell.

Police Judge.—John G. Hatch.

Street Commissioner and Marshal.—James Nicholson.

City Clerk.—Samuel I. Lorah.

Surveyor.—John D. Peregrine.

City Attorney.—Harper M. Orahood.

Aldermen.—First Ward, Wm. Lehmkuhl, Peter McFarlane; Second Ward, A. Bitzenhofer, S. B. Hahn; Third Ward, N. H. McCall, Marcus Leahy; Fourth Ward, Alex. Carstens, Thomas Hambley.

School Board.—S. B. Hahn, (president,) H. M. Teller, Chas. F. Hendrie, F. C. Young, Bart. Robins.

BLACK HAWK—MUNICIPAL.

Mayor.—John B. Ballard.
Police Judge.—Robert S. Haight.
Treasurer.—I. Turp. Graham.
Assessor.—Thomas J. Oyler.
Clerk.—Robert S. Haight.
Marshal and Street Commissioner.—James L. Chapline.
Attorney.—Alvin Marsh.
Aldermen.—First Ward, Fred. A. Rudolph, J. F. McNair; Second Ward, E. S. Blake, C. Strasburg; Third Ward, H. W. Lake, Henry Hartman.
School Board.—The City Council.

NEVADAVILLE—TOWN.

Trustees—James Noonan, R. B. Williams, Richard Hansckle, L. L. Roberts, A. W. Tucker.
Town Clerk.—John J. Clark.
Constable and Supervisor.—George Sparks.

DENVER MIRROR.

Devoted to Mining News, General Intelligence from all parts of the Country, and Politics.

—PUBLISHED EVERY SUNDAY MORNING AT—

391 Lawrence Street, - Denver, Colorado.

SUBSCRIPTION RATES:

One copy one year, $2.20. One copy six months, $1.35.

Address, STANLEY G. FOWLER.

POLLOCK'S LIVERY STABLE,

CENTRAL CITY, - COLORADO.

Carriages, Saddle Horses, and Turn-outs of every description furnished on short notice. Tourists and others visiting Central can depend on securing the best outfits at reasonable rates.

Parties can secure conveyances by telegraph, which will be found at the C. C. R. R. depot upon the arrival of the train.

2d door west of TELLER HOUSE.

JOSEPH TISHLER,

CALIFORNIA FRUIT STORE,

Central City, Colorado.

Fruits, Confectionery, Cigars and Tobacco.

—THE—
O. K. STORE

—LARGEST AND MOST COMPLETE STOCK OF—

Fashionable Clothing

—AND—

GENT'S FINE FURNISHING GOODS

ALWAYS ON HAND.

Introducers of latest novelties in our line.

Prices always low down and within the reach of everybody. Your trade is solicited, and an inspection of our stock earnestly requested.

A. JACOBS & CO.

GOLD RUSH BOOKS

OREGON, USA

www.GoldMiningBooks.com

Books On Mining

Visit: www.goldminingbooks.com to order your copies or ask your favorite book seller to offer them.

Mining Books by Kerby Jackson

<u>Gold Dust: Stories From Oregon's Mining Years</u> - Oregon mining historian and prospector, Kerby Jackson, brings you a treasure trove of seventeen stories on Southern Oregon's rich history of gold prospecting, the prospectors and their discoveries, and the breathtaking areas they settled in and made homes. 5" X 8", 98 ppgs. Retail Price: $11.99

<u>The Golden Trail: More Stories From Oregon's Mining Years</u> - In his follow-up to "Gold Dust: Stories of Oregon's Mining Years", this time around, Jackson brings us twelve tales from Oregon's Gold Rush, including the story about the first gold strike on Canyon Creek in Grant County, about the old timers who found gold by the pail full at the Victor Mine near Galice, how Iradel Bray discovered a rich ledge of gold on the Coquille River during the height of the Rogue River War, a tale of two elderly miners on the hunt for a lost mine in the Cascade Mountains, details about the discovery of the famous Armstrong Nugget and others. 5" X 8", 70 ppgs. Retail Price: $10.99

Oregon Mining Books

<u>Geology and Mineral Resources of Josephine County, Oregon</u> - Unavailable since the 1970's, this important publication was originally compiled by the Oregon Department of Geology and Mineral Industries and includes important details on the economic geology and mineral resources of this important mining area in South Western Oregon. Included are notes on the history, geology and development of important mines, as well as insights into the mining of gold, copper, nickel, limestone, chromium and other minerals found in large quantities in Josephine County, Oregon. 8.5" X 11", 54 ppgs. Retail Price: $9.99

<u>Mines and Prospects of the Mount Reuben Mining District</u> - Unavailable since 1947, this important publication was originally compiled by geologist Elton Youngberg of the Oregon Department of Geology and Mineral Industries and includes detailed descriptions, histories and the geology of the Mount Reuben Mining District in Josephine County, Oregon. Included are notes on the history, geology, development and assay statistics, as well as underground maps of all the major mines and prospects in the vicinity of this much neglected mining district. 8.5" X 11", 48 ppgs. Retail Price: $9.99

<u>The Granite Mining District</u> - Notes on the history, geology and development of important mines in the well known Granite Mining District which is located in Grant County, Oregon. Some of the mines discussed include the Ajax, Blue Ribbon, Buffalo, Continental, Cougar-Independence, Magnolia, New York, Standard and the Tillicum. Also included are many rare maps pertaining to the mines in the area. 8.5" X 11", 48 ppgs. Retail Price: $9.99

<u>Ore Deposits of the Takilma and Waldo Mining Districts of Josephine County, Oregon</u> - The Waldo and Takilma mining districts are most notable for the fact that the earliest large scale mining of placer gold and copper in Oregon took place in these two areas. Included are details about some of the earliest large gold mines in the state such as the Llano de Oro, High Gravel, Cameron, Platerica, Deep Gravel and others, as well as copper mines such as the famous Queen of Bronze mine, the Waldo, Lily and Cowboy mines. This volume also includes six maps and 20 original illustrations. 8.5" X 11", 74 ppgs. Retail Price: $9.99

<u>Metal Mines of Douglas, Coos and Curry Counties, Oregon</u> - Oregon mining historian Kerby Jackson introduces us to a classic work on Oregon's mining history in this important re-issue of Bulletin 14C Volume 1, otherwise known as the Douglas, Coos & Curry Counties, Oregon Metal Mines Handbook. Unavailable since 1940, this important publication was originally compiled by the Oregon Department of Geology and Mineral Industries includes detailed descriptions, histories and the geology of over 250 metallic mineral mines and prospects in this rugged area of South West Oregon. 8.5" X 11", 158 ppgs. Retail Price: $19.99

Metal Mines of Jackson County, Oregon - Unavailable since 1943, this important publication was originally compiled by the Oregon Department of Geology and Mineral Industries includes detailed descriptions, histories and the geology of over 450 metallic mineral mines and prospects in Jackson County, Oregon. Included are such famous gold mining areas as Gold Hill, Jacksonville, Sterling and the Upper Applegate. **8.5" X 11", 220 ppgs. Retail Price: $24.99**

Metal Mines of Josephine County, Oregon - Oregon mining historian Kerby Jackson introduces us to a classic work on Oregon's mining history in this important re-issue of Bulletin 14C, otherwise known as the Josephine County, Oregon Metal Mines Handbook. Unavailable since 1952, this important publication was originally compiled by the Oregon Department of Geology and Mineral Industries includes detailed descriptions, histories and the geology of over 500 metallic mineral mines and prospects in Josephine County, Oregon. **8.5" X 11", 250 ppgs. Retail Price: $24.99**

Metal Mines of North East Oregon - Oregon mining historian Kerby Jackson introduces us to a classic work on Oregon's mining history in this important re-issue of Bulletin 14A and 14B, otherwise known as the North East Oregon Metal Mines Handbook. Unavailable since 1941, this important publication was originally compiled by the Oregon Department of Geology and Mineral Industries and includes detailed descriptions, histories and the geology of over 750 metallic mineral mines and prospects in North Eastern Oregon. **8.5" X 11", 310 ppgs. Retail Price: $29.99**

Metal Mines of North West Oregon - Oregon mining historian Kerby Jackson introduces us to a classic work on Oregon's mining history in this important re-issue of Bulletin 14D, otherwise known as the North West Oregon Metal Mines Handbook. Unavailable since 1951, this important publication was originally compiled by the Oregon Department of Geology and Mineral Industries and includes detailed descriptions, histories and the geology of over 250 metallic mineral mines and prospects in North Western Oregon. **8.5" X 11", 182 ppgs. Retail Price: $19.99**

Mines and Prospects of Oregon - Mining historian Kerby Jackson introduces us to a classic mining work by the Oregon Bureau of Mines in this important re-issue of The Handbook of Mines and Prospects of Oregon. Unavailable since 1916, this publication includes important insights into hundreds of gold, silver, copper, coal, limestone and other mines that operated in the State of Oregon around the turn of the 19th Century. Included are not only geological details on early mines throughout Oregon, but also insights into their history, production, locations and in some cases, also included are rare maps of their underground workings. **8.5" X 11", 314 ppgs. Retail Price: $24.99**

Lode Gold of the Klamath Mountains of Northern California and South West Oregon
(See California Mining Books)

Mineral Resources of South West Oregon - Unavailable since 1914, this publication includes important insights into dozens of mines that once operated in South West Oregon, including the famous gold fields of Josephine and Jackson Counties, as well as the Coal Mines of Coos County. Included are not only geological details on early mines throughout South West Oregon, but also insights into their history, production and locations. **8.5" X 11", 154 ppgs. Retail Price: $11.99**

Chromite Mining in The Klamath Mountains of California and Oregon
(See California Mining Books)

Southern Oregon Mineral Wealth - Unavailable since 1904, this rare publication provides a unique snapshot into the mines that were operating in the area at the time. Included are not only geological details on early mines throughout South West Oregon, but also insights into their history, production and locations. Some of the mining areas include Grave Creek, Greenback, Wolf Creek, Jump Off Joe Creek, Granite Hill, Galice, Mount Reuben, Gold Hill, Galls Creek, Kane Creek, Sardine Creek, Birdseye Creek, Evans Creek, Foots Creek, Jacksonville, Ashland, the Applegate River, Waldo, Kerby and the Illinois River, Althouse and Sucker Creek, as well as insights into local copper mining and other topics. **8.5" X 11", 64 ppgs. Retail Price: $8.99**

Geology and Ore Deposits of the Takilma and Waldo Mining Districts - Unavailable since the 1933, this publication was originally compiled by the United States Geological Survey and includes details on gold and copper mining in the Takilma and Waldo Districts of Josephine County, Oregon. The Waldo and Takilma mining districts are most notable for the fact that the earliest large scale mining of placer gold and copper in Oregon took place in these two areas. Included in this report are details about some of the earliest large gold mines in the state such as the Llano de Oro, High Gravel, Cameron, Platerica, Deep Gravel and others, as well as copper mines such as the famous Queen of Bronze mine, the Waldo, Lily and Cowboy mines. In addition to geological examinations, insights are also provided into the production, day to day operations and early histories of these mines, as well as calculations of known mineral reserves in the area. This volume also includes six maps and 20 original illustrations. **8.5" X 11", 74 ppgs. Retail Price: $9.99**

Gold Mines of Oregon - Oregon mining historian Kerby Jackson introduces us to a classic work on Oregon's mining history in this important re-issue of Bulletin 61, otherwise known as "Gold and Silver In Oregon". Unavailable since 1968, this important publication was originally compiled by geologists Howard C. Brooks and Len Ramp of the Oregon Department of Geology and Mineral Industries and includes detailed descriptions, histories and the geology of over 450 gold mines Oregon. Included are notes on the history, geology and gold production statistics of all the major mining areas in Oregon including the Klamath Mountains, the Blue Mountains and the North Cascades. While gold is where you find it, as every miner knows, the path to success is to prospect for gold where it was previously found. **8.5" X 11", 344 ppgs. Retail Price: $24.99**

Mines and Mineral Resources of Curry County Oregon - Originally published in 1916, this important publication on Oregon Mining has not been available for nearly a century. Included are rare insights into the history, production and locations of dozens of gold mines in Curry County, Oregon, as well as detailed information on important Oregon mining districts in that area such as those at Agness, Bald Face Creek, Mule Creek, Boulder Creek, China Diggings, Collier Creek, Elk River, Gold Beach, Rock Creek, Sixes River and elsewhere. Particular attention is especially paid to the famous beach gold deposits of this portion of the Oregon Coast. **8.5" X 11", 140 ppgs. Retail Price: $11.99**

Chromite Mining in South West Oregon - Originally published in 1961, this important publication on Oregon Mining has not been available for nearly a century. Included are rare insights into the history, production and locations of nearly 300 chromite mines in South Western Oregon. **8.5" X 11", 184 ppgs. Retail Price: $14.99**

Mineral Resources of Douglas County Oregon - Originally published in 1972, this important publication on Oregon Mining has not been available for nearly forty years. Included are rare insights into the geology, history, production and locations of numerous gold mines and other mining properties in Douglas County, Oregon. **8.5" X 11", 124 ppgs. Retail Price: $11.99**

Mineral Resources of Coos County Oregon - Originally published in 1972, this important publication on Oregon Mining has not been available for nearly forty years. Included are rare insights into the geology, history, production and locations of numerous gold mines and other mining properties in Coos County, Oregon. **8.5" X 11", 100 ppgs. Retail Price: $11.99**

Mineral Resources of Lane County Oregon - Originally published in 1938, this important publication on Oregon Mining has not been available for nearly seventy five years. Included are extremely rare insights into the geology and mines of Lane County, Oregon, in particular in the Bohemia, Blue River, Oakridge, Black Butte and Winberry Mining Districts. **8.5" X 11", 82 ppgs. Retail Price: $9.99**

Mineral Resources of the Upper Chetco River of Oregon: Including the Kalmiopsis Wilderness - Originally published in 1975, this important publication on Oregon Mining has not been available for nearly forty years. Withdrawn under the 1872 Mining Act since 1984, real insight into the minerals resources and mines of the Upper Chetco River has long been unavailable due to the remoteness of the area. Despite this, the decades of battle between property owners and environmental extremists over the last private mining inholding in the area has continued to pique the interest of those interested in mining and other forms of natural resource use. Gold mining began in the area in the 1850's and has a rich history in this geographic area, even if the facts surrounding it are little known. Included are twenty two rare photographs, as well as insights into the Becca and Morning Mine, the Emmly Mine (also known as Emily Camp), the Frazier Mine, the Golden Dream or Higgins Mine, Hustis Mine, Peck Mine and others. **8.5" X 11", 64 ppgs. Retail Price: $8.99**

Gold Dredging in Oregon - Originally published in 1939, this important publication on Oregon Mining has not been available for nearly seventy five years. Included are extremely rare insights into the history and day to day operations of the dragline and bucketline gold dredges that once worked the placer gold fields of South West and North East Oregon in decades gone by. Also included are details in the areas that were worked by gold dredges in Josephine, Jackson, Baker and Grant counties, as well as the economic factors that impacted this mining method. This volume also offers a unique look into the values of river bottom land in relation to both farming and mining, in how farm lands were mined, re-soiled and reclamated after the dredges worked them. Featured are hard to find maps of the gold dredge fields, as well as rare photographs from a bygone era. **8.5" X 11", 86 ppgs. Retail Price: $8.99**

Quick Silver Mining in Oregon - Originally published in 1963, this important publication on Oregon Mining has not been available for over fifty years. This publication includes details into the history and production of Elemental Mercury or Quicksilver in the State of Oregon. **8.5" X 11", 238 ppgs. Retail Price: $15.99**

Mines of the Greenhorn Mining District of Grant County Oregon - Originally published in 1948, this important publication on Oregon Mining has not been available for over sixty five years. In this publication are rare insights into the mines of the famous Greenhorn Mining District of Grant County, Oregon, especially the famous Morning Mine. Also included are details on the Tempest, Tiger, Bi-Metallic, Windsor, Psyche, Big Johnny, Snow Creek, Banzette and Paramount Mines, as well as prospects in the vicinities in the famous mining areas of Mormon Basin, Vinegar Basin and Desolation Creek. Included are hard to find mine maps and dozens of rare photographs from the bygone era of Grant County's rich mining history. **8.5" X 11", 72 ppgs. Retail Price: $9.99**

Geology of the Wallowa Mountains of Oregon: Part I (Volume 1) - Originally published in 1938, this important publication on Oregon Mining has not been available for nearly seventy five years. Included are details on the geology of this unique portion of North Eastern Oregon. This is the first part of a two book series on the area. Accompanying the text are rare photographs and historic maps. 8.5" X 11", 92 ppgs. Retail Price: $9.99

Geology of the Wallowa Mountains of Oregon: Part II (Volume 2) - Originally published in 1938, this important publication on Oregon Mining has not been available for nearly seventy five years. Included are details on the geology of this unique portion of North Eastern Oregon. This is the first part of a two book series on the area. Accompanying the text are rare photographs and historic maps. 8.5" X 11", 94 ppgs. Retail Price: $9.99

Field Identification of Minerals For Oregon Prospectors - Originally published in 1940, this important publication on Oregon Mining has not been available for nearly seventy five years. Included in this volume is an easy system for testing and identifying a wide range of minerals that might be found by prospectors, geologists and rockhounds in the State of Oregon, as well as in other locales. Topics include how to put together your own field testing kit and how to conduct rudimentary tests in the field. This volume is written in a clear and concise way to make it useful even for beginners. 8.5" X 11", 158 ppgs. Retail Price: $14.99

The Bohemia Mining District of Oregon - Originally published in 1900, this important publication on Oregon Mining has not been available for over a century. Included in this volume are important insights into the famous Bohemia Mining District of Oregon, including the histories and locations of important gold mines in the area such as the Ophir Mine, Clarence, Acturas, Peek-a-boo, White Swan, Combination Mine, the Musick Mine, The California, White Ghost, The Mystery, Wall Street, Vesuvius, Story, Lizzie Bullock, Delta, Elsie Dora, Golden Slipper, Broadway, Champion Mine, Knott, Noonday, Helena, White Wings, Riverside and others. Also included are notes on the nearby Blue River Mining District. 8.5" X 11", 58 ppgs. Retail Price: $9.99

The Gold Fields of Eastern Oregon - Unavailable since 1900, this publication was originally compiled by the Baker City Chamber of Commerce Offering important insights into the gold mining history of Eastern Oregon, "The Gold Fields of Eastern Oregon" sheds a rare light on many of the gold mines that were operating at the turn of the 19th Century in Baker County and Grant County in North Eastern Oregon. Some of the areas featured include the Cable Cove District, Baisely-Elhorn, Granite, Red Boy, Bonanza, Susanville, Sparta, Virtue, Vaughn, Sumpter, Burnt River, Rye Valley and other mining districts. Included is basic information on not only many gold mines that are well known to those interested in Eastern Oregon mining history, but also many mines and prospects which have been mostly lost to the passage of time. Accompanying are numerous rare photos 8.5" X 11", 78 ppgs. Retail Price: $10.99

Idaho Mining Books

Gold in Idaho - Unavailable since the 1940's, this publication was originally compiled by the Idaho Bureau of Mines and includes details on gold mining in Idaho. Included is not only raw data on gold production in Idaho, but also valuable insight into where gold may be found in Idaho, as well as practical information on the gold bearing rocks and other geological features that will assist those looking for placer and lode gold in the State of Idaho. This volume also includes thirteen gold maps that greatly enhance the practical usability of the information contained in this small book detailing where to find gold in Idaho. 8.5" X 11", 72 ppgs. Retail Price: $9.99

Geology of the Couer D'Alene Mining District of Idaho - Unavailable since 1961, this publication was originally compiled by the Idaho Bureau of Mines and Geology and includes details on the mining of gold, silver and other minerals in the famous Coeur D'Alene Mining District in Northern Idaho. Included are details on the early history of the Coeur D'Alene Mining District, local tectonic settings, ore deposit features, information on the mineral belts of the Osburn Fault, as well as detailed information on the famous Bunker Hill Mine, the Dayrock Mine, Galena Mine, Lucky Friday Mine and the infamous Sunshine Mine. This volume also includes sixteen hard to find maps. 8.5" X 11", 70 ppgs. Retail Price: $9.99

The Gold Camps and Silver Cities of Idaho - Originally published in 1963, this important publication on Idaho Mining has not been available for nearly fifty years. Included are rare insights into the history of Idaho's Gold Rush, as well as the mad craze for silver in the Idaho Panhandle. Documented in fine detail are the early mining excitements at Boise Basin, at South Boise, in the Owyhees, at Deadwood, Long Valley, Stanley Basin and Robinson Bar, at Atlanta, on the famous Boise River, Volcano, Little Smokey, Banner, Boise Ridge, Hailey, Leesburg, Lemhi, Pearl, at South Mountain, Shoup and Ulysses, Yellow Jacket and Loon Creek. The story follows with the appearance of Chinese miners at the new mining camps on the Snake River, Black Pine, Yankee Fork, Bay Horse, Clayton, Heath, Seven Devils, Gibbonsville, Vienna and Sawtooth City. Also included are special sections on the Idaho Lead and Silver mines of the late 1800's, as well as the mining discoveries of the early 1900's that paved the way for Idaho's modern mining and mineral industry. Lavishly illustrated with rare historic photos, this volume provides a one of a kind documentary into Idaho's mining history that is sure to be enjoyed by not only modern miners and prospectors who still scour the hills in search of nature's treasures, but also those enjoy history and tromping through overgrown ghost towns and long abandoned mining camps. 8.5" X 11", 186 ppgs. Retail Price: $14.99

Ore Deposits and Mining in North Western Custer County Idaho - Unavailable since 1913, this important publication was originally published by the Us Department of the Interior and has been unavailable for a century. Included are fine details on the geology, geography, gold placers and gold and silver bearing quartz veins of the mining region of North West Custer County, Idaho. Of particular interest is a rare look at the mines and prospects of the region, including those such as the Ramshorn Mine, SkyLark, Riverview, Excelsior, Beardsley, Pacific, Hoosier, Silver Brick, Forest Rose and dozens of others in the Bay Horse Mining District. Also covered are the mines of the Yankee Fork District such as the Lucky Boy, Badger, Black, Enterprise, Charles Dickens, Morrison, Golden Sunbeam, Montana, Golden Gate and others, as well as those in the Loon Mining District. **8.5" X 11", 126 ppgs. Retail Price: $12.99**

Gold Rush To Idaho - Unavailable since 1963, this important publication was originally published by the Idaho Bureau of Mines and has been unavailable for 50 years. "Gold Rush To Idaho" revisits the earliest years of the discovery of gold in Idaho Territory and introduces us to the conditions that the pioneer gold seekers met when they blazed a trail through the wilderness of Idaho's mountains and discovered the precious yellow metal at Oro Fino and Pierce. Subsequent rushes followed at places like Elk City, Newsome, Clearwater Station, Florence, Warrens and elsewhere. Of particular interest is a rare look at the hardships that the first miners in Idaho met with during their day to day existences and their attempts to bring law and order to their mining camps. **8.5" X 11", 88 ppgs. Retail Price: $9.99**

The Geology and Mines of Northern Idaho and North Western Montana - Unavailable since 1909, this important publication was originally published by the Us Department of the Interior and has been unavailable for a century. Included are fine details on the geology and geography of the mining regions of Northern Idaho and North Western Montana. Of particular interest is a rare look at the mines and prospects of the region, including those in the Pine Creek Mining District, Lake Pend Oreille district, Troy Mining District, Sylvanite District, Cabinet Mining District, Prospect Mining District and the Missoula Valley. Some of the mines featured include the Iron Mountain, Silver Butte, Snowshoe, Grouse Mountain Mine and others. **8.5" X 11", 142 ppgs. Retail Price: $12.99**

Utah Mining Books

Fluorite in Utah - Unavailable since 1954, this publication was originally compiled by the USGS, State of Utah and U.S. Atomic Energy Commission and details the mining of fluorspar, also known as fluorite in the State of Utah. Included are details on the geology and history of fluorspar (fluorite) mining in Utah, including details on where this unique gem mineral may be found in the State of Utah. **8.5" X 11", 60 ppgs. Retail Price: $8.99**

California Mining Books

The Tertiary Gravels of the Sierra Nevada of California - Mining historian Kerby Jackson introduces us to a classic mining work by Waldemar Lindgren in this important re-issue of The Tertiary Gravels of the Sierra Nevada of California. Unavailable since 1911, this publication includes details on the gold bearing ancient river channels of the famous Sierra Nevada region of California. **8.5" X 11", 282 ppgs. Retail Price: $19.99**

The Mother Lode Mining Region of California - Unavailable since 1900, this publication includes details on the gold mines of California's famous Mother Lode gold mining area. Included are details on the geology, history and important gold mines of the region, as well as insights into historic mining methods, mine timbering, mining machinery, mining bell signals and other details on how these mines operated. Also included are insights into the gold mines of the California Mother Lode that were in operation during the first sixty years of California's mining history. **8.5" X 11", 176 ppgs. Retail Price: $14.99**

Lode Gold of the Klamath Mountains of Northern California and South West Oregon - Unavailable since 1971, this publication was originally compiled by Preston E. Hotz and includes details on the lode mining districts of Oregon and California's Klamath Mountains. Included are details on the geology, history and important lode mines of the French Gulch, Deadwood, Whiskeytown, Shasta, Redding, Muletown, South Fork, Old Diggings, Dog Creek (Delta), Bully Choop (Indian Creek), Harrison Gulch, Hayfork, Minersville, Trinity Center, Canyon Creek, East Fork, New River, Denny, Liberty (Black Bear), Cecilville, Callahan, Yreka, Fort Jones and Happy Camp mining districts in California, as well as the Ashland, Rogue River, Applegate, Illinois River, Takilma, Greenback, Galice, Silver Peak, Myrtle Creek and Mule Creek districts of South Western Oregon. Also included are insights into the mineralization and other characteristics of this important mining region. **8.5" X 11", 100 ppgs. Retail Price: $10.99**

Mines and Mineral Resources of Shasta County, Siskiyou County, Trinity County: California - Unavailable since 1915, this publication was originally compiled by the California State Mining Bureau and includes details on the gold mines of this area of Northern California. Also included are insights into the mineralization and other characteristics of this important mining region, as well as the location of historic gold mines. **8.5" X 11", 204 ppgs. Retail Price: $19.99**

Geology of the Yreka Quadrangle, Siskiyou County, California - Unavailable since 1977, this publication was originally compiled by Preston E. Hotz and includes details on the geology of the Yreka Quadrangle of Siskiyou County, California. Also included are insights into the mineralization and other characteristics of this important mining region. **8.5" X 11", 78 ppgs. Retail Price: $7.99**

Mines of San Diego and Imperial Counties, California - Originally published in 1914, this important publication on California Mining has not been available for a century. This publication includes important information on the early gold mines of San Diego and Imperial County, which were some of the first gold fields mined in California by early Spanish and Mexican miners before the 49ers came on the scene. Included are not only details on early mining methods in the area, production statistics and geological information, but also the location of the early gold mines that helped make California "The Golden State". Also included are details on the mining of other minerals such as silver, lead, zinc, manganese, tungsten, vanadium, asbestos, barite, borax, cement, clay, dolomite, fluospar, gem stones, graphite, marble, salines, petroleum, stronium, talc and others. **8.5" X 11", 116 ppgs. Retail Price: $12.99**

Mines of Sierra County, California - Unavailable since 1920, this publication was originally compiled by the California State Mining Bureau and includes details on the gold mines of Sierra County, California. Also included are insights into the mineralization and other characteristics of this important mining region, as well as the location of historic gold mines. **8.5" X 11", 156 ppgs. Retail Price: $19.99**

Mines of Plumas County, California - Unavailable since 1918, this publication was originally compiled by the California State Mining Bureau and includes details on the gold mines of Plumas County, California. Also included are insights into the mineralization and other characteristics of this important mining region, as well as the location of historic gold mines. **8.5" X 11", 200 ppgs. Retail Price: $19.99**

Mines of El Dorado, Placer, Sacramento and Yuba Counties, California - Originally published in 1917, this important publication on California Mining has not been available for nearly a century. This publication includes important information on the early gold mines of El Dorado County, Placer County, Sacramento County and Yuba County, which were some of the first gold fields mined by the Forty-Niners during the California Gold Rush. Included are not only details on early mining methods in the area, production statistics and geological information, but also the location of the early gold mines that helped make California "The Golden State". Also included are insights into the early mining of chrome, copper and other minerals in this important mining area. **8.5" X 11", 204 ppgs. Retail Price: $19.99**

Mines of Los Angeles, Orange and Riverside Counties, California - Originally published in 1917, this important publication on California Mining has not been available for nearly a century. This publication includes important information on the early gold mines of Los Angeles County, Orange County and Riverside County, which were some of the first gold fields mined in California by early Spanish and Mexican miners before the 49ers came on the scene. Included are not only details on early mining methods in the area, production statistics and geological information, but also the location of the early gold mines that helped make California "The Golden State". **8.5" X 11", 146 ppgs. Retail Price: $12.99**

Mines of San Bernadino and Tulare Counties, California - Originally published in 1917, this important publication on California Mining has not been available for nearly a century. This publication includes important information on the early gold mines of San Bernadino and Tulare County, which were some of the first gold fields mined in California by early Spanish and Mexican miners before the 49ers came on the scene. Included are not only details on early mining methods in the area, production statistics and geological information, but also the location of the early gold mines that helped make California "The Golden State". Also included are details on the mining of other minerals such as copper, iron, lead, zinc, manganese, tungsten, vanadium, asbestos, barite, borax, cement, clay, dolomite, fluospar, gem stones, graphite, marble, salines, petroleum, stronium, talc and others. **8.5" X 11", 200 ppgs. Retail Price: $19.99**

Chromite Mining in The Klamath Mountains of California and Oregon - Unavailable since 1919, this publication was originally compiled by J.S. Diller of the United States Department of Geological Survey and includes details on the chromite mines of this area of Northern California and Southern Oregon. Also included are insights into the mineralization and other characteristics of this important mining region, as well as the location of historic mines. Also included are insights into chromite mining in Eastern Oregon and Montana. **8.5" X 11", 98 ppgs. Retail Price: $9.99**

Mines and Mining in Amador, Calaveras and Tuolumne Counties, California - Unavailable since 1915, this publication was originally compiled by William Tucker and includes details on the mines and mineral resources of this important California mining area. Included are details on the geology, history and important gold mines of the region, as well as insights into other local mineral resources such as asbestos, clay, copper, talc, limestone and others. Also included are insights into the mineralization and other characteristics of this important portion of California's Mother Lode mining region. **8.5" X 11", 198 ppgs. Retail Price: $14.99**

The Cerro Gordo Mining District of Inyo County California - Unavailable since 1963, this publication was originally compiled by the United States Department of Interior. Included are insights into the mineralization and other characteristics of this important mining region of Southern California. Topics include the mining of gold and silver in this important mining district in Inyo County, California, including details on the history, production and locations of the Cerro Gordo Mine, the Morning Star Mine, Estelle Tunnel, Charles Lease Tunnel, Ignacio, Hart, Crosscut Tunnel, Sunset, Upper Newtown, Newtown, Ella, Perseverance, Newsboy, Belmont and other silver and gold mines in the Cerro Gordo Mining District. This volume also includes important insights into the fossil record, geologic formations, faults and other aspects of economic geology in this California mining district. **8.5" X 11", 104 ppgs.** Retail Price: $10.99

Mining in Butte, Lassen, Modoc, Sutter and Tehama Counties of California - Unavailable since 1917, this publication was originally compiled by the United States Department of Interior. Included are insights into the mineralization and other characteristics of this important mining region of California. Topics include the mining of asbestos, chromite, gold, diamonds and manganese in Butte County, the mining of gold and copper in the Hayden Hill and Diamond Mountain mining districts of Lassen County, the mining of coal, salt, copper and gold in the High Grade and Winters mining districts of Modoc County, gold mining in Sutter County and the mining of gold, chromite, manganese and copper in Tehama County. This volume also includes the production records and locations of numerous mines in this important mining region. **8.5" X 11", 114 ppgs. Retail Price: $11.99**

Mines of Trinity County California - Originally published in 1965, this important publication on California Mining has not been available for nearly fifty years. This publication includes important information on mines and mining in Trinity County, California, as well insights into the mineralization and geology of this important mining area in Northern California. Included are extensive details on hardrock and placer gold mines and prospects, including charts showing the locations of these historic mines.. **8.5" X 11", 144 ppgs. Retail Price: $12.99**

Mines of Kern County California - Originally published in 1962, this important publication on California Mining has not been available for nearly fifty years. This publication includes important information on mines and mining in Kern County, California, as well insights into the mineralization and geology of this important mining area in California. Included are extensive details on hardrock and placer gold mines and prospects, including charts showing the locations of these historic mines. **8.5" X 11", 398 ppgs. Retail Price: $24.99**

Mines of Calaveras County California - Originally published in 1962, this important publication on California Mining has not been available for nearly fifty years. This publication includes important information on mines and mining in Calaveras County, California, as well insights into the mineralization and geology of this important mining area in Northern California. Included are extensive details on hardrock and placer gold mines and prospects, including charts showing the locations of these historic mines. **8.5" X 11", 236 ppgs. Retail Price: $19.99**

Lode Gold Mining in Grass Valley California - Unavailable since 1940, this publication was originally compiled by the United States Department of Interior. Included are insights into the gold mineralization and other characteristics of this important mining region of Nevada County, California. This volume also includes important insights into the geologic formations, faults and other aspects of economic geology in this California mining district. Of particular interest are the fine details on many hardrock gold mines in the area, including their locations, histories, development and mineralization. Some of the mines featured include the Gold Hill Mine, Massachusetts Hill, Boundary, Peabody, Golden Center, North Star, Omaha, Lone Jack, Homeward Bound, Hartery, Wisconsin, Allison Ranch, Phoenix, Kate Hayes, W.Y.O.D., Empire, Rich Hill, Daisy Hill, Orleans, Sultana, Centennial, Conlin, Ben Franklin, Crown Point and many others. **8.5" X 11", 148 ppgs. Retail Price: $12.99**

Alaska Mining Books

Ore Deposits of the Willow Creek Mining District, Alaska - Unavailable since 1954, this hard to find publication includes valuable insights into the Willow Creek Mining District near Hatcher Pass in Alaska. The publication includes insights into the history, geology and locations of the well known mines in the area, including the Gold Cord, Independence, Fern, Mabel, Lonesome, Snowbird, Schroff-O'Neil, High Grade, Marion Twin, Thorpe, Webfoot, Kelly-Willow, Lane, Holland and others. **8.5" X 11", 96 ppgs. Retail Price: $9.99**

Arizona Mining Books

Mines and Mining in Northern Yuma County Arizona - Originally published in 1911, this important publication on Arizona Mining has not been available for over a hundred years. Included are rare insights into the gold, silver, copper and quicksilver mines of Yuma County, Arizona together with hard to find maps and photographs. Some of the mines and mining districts featured include the Planet Copper Mine, Mineral Hill, the Clara Consolidated Mine, Viati Mine, Copper Basin prospect, Bowman Mine, Quartz King, Billy Mack, Carnation, the Wardwell and Osbourne, Valensuella Copper, the Mariquita, Colonial Mine, the French American, the New York-Plomosa, Guadalupe, Lead Camp, Mudersbach Copper Camp, Yellow Bird, the Arizona Northern (Salome Strike), Bonanza (Harqua Hala), Golden Eagle, Hercules, Socorro and others. **8.5" X 11", 144 ppgs. Retail Price: $11.99**

The Aravaipa and Stanley Mining Districts of Graham County Arizona - Originally published in 1925, this important publication on Arizona Mining has not been available for nearly ninety years. Included are rare insights into the gold and silver mines of these two important mining districts, together with hard to find maps. **8.5" X 11", 140 ppgs. Retail Price: $11.99**

Gold in the Gold Basin and Lost Basin Mining Districts of Mohave County, Arizona - This volume contains rare insights into the geology and gold mineralization of the Gold Basin and Lost Basin Mining Districts of Mohave County, Arizona that will be of benefit to miners and prospectors. Also included is a significant body of information on the gold mines and prospects of this portion of Arizona. This volume is lavishly illustrated with rare photos and mining maps. **8.5" X 11", 188 ppgs. Retail Price: $19.99**

Mines of the Jerome and Bradshaw Mountains of Arizona - This important publication on Arizona Mining has not been available for ninety years. This volume contains rare insights into the geology and ore deposits of the Jerome and Bradshaw Mountains of Arizona that will be of benefit to miners and prospectors who work those areas. Included is a significant body of information on the mines and prospects of the Verde, Black Hills, Cherry Creek, Prescott, Walker, Groom Creek, Hassayampa, Bigbug, Turkey Creek, Agua Fria, Black Canyon, Peck, Tiger, Pine Grove, Bradshaw, Tintop, Humbug and Castle Creek Mining Districts. This volume is lavishly illustrated with rare photos and mining maps. **8.5" X 11", 218 ppgs. Retail Price: $19.99**

The Ajo Mining District of Pima County Arizona - This important publication on Arizona Mining has not been available for nearly seventy years. This volume contains rare insights into the geology and mineralization of the Ajo Mining District in Pima County, Arizona and in particular the famous New Cornelia Mine. **8.5" X 11", 126 ppgs. Retail Price: $11.99**

Mining in the Santa Rita and Patagonia Mountains of Arizona - Originally published in 1915, this important publication on Arizona Mining has not been available for nearly a century. Included are rare insights into hundreds of gold, silver, copper and other mines in this famous Arizona mining area. Details include the locations, geology, history, production and other facts of the mines of this region. **8.5" X 11", 394 ppgs. Retail Price: $24.99**

Montana Mining Books

A History of Butte Montana: The World's Greatest Mining Camp - First published in 1900 by H.C. Freeman, this important publication sheds a bright light on one of the most important mining areas in the history of The West. Together with his insights, as well as rare photographs of the periods, Harry Freeman describes Butte and its vicinity from its early beginnings, right up to its flush years when copper flowed from its mines like a river. At the time of publication, Butte, Montana was known worldwide as "The Richest Mining Spot On Earth" and produced not only vast amounts of copper, but also silver, gold and other metals from its mines. Freeman illustrates, with great detail, the most important mines in the vicinity of Butte, providing rare details on their owners, their history and most importantly, how the mines operated and how their treasures were extracted. Of particular interest are the dozens of rare photographs that depict mines such as the famous Anaconda, the Silver Bow, the Smoke House, Moose, Paulin, Buffalo, Little Minah, the Mountain Consolidated, West Greyrock, Cora, the Green Mountain, Diamond, Bell, Parnell, the Neversweat, Nipper, Original and many others. **8.5" X 11", 142 ppgs. Retail Price: $12.99**

The Butte Mining District of Montana - This important publication on Montana Mining has not been available for over a century. Included are rare insights into the gold, copper and silver mines of Butte, Montana together with hard to find maps and photographs. Some of the topics include the early history of gold, silver and copper mining in the Butte area, insight into the geology of its mining areas, the local distribution of gold, silver and copper ores, as well their composition and how to identify them. Also included are detailed facts about the mines in the Butte Mining District, including the famous Anaconda Mine, Gagnon, Parrot, Blue Vein, Moscow, Poulin, Stella, Buffalo, Green Mountain, Wake Up Jim, the Diamond-Bell Group, Mountain Consolidated, East Greyrock, West Greyrock, Snowball, Corra, Speculator, Adirondack, Miners Union, the Jessie-Edith May Group, Otisco, Iduna, Colorado, Lizzie, Cambers, Anderson, Hesperus, Preferencia and dozens of others. **8.5" X 11", 298 ppgs. Retail Price: $24.99**

Mines of the Helena Mining Region of Montana - This important publication on Montana Mining has not been available for over a century. Included are rare insights into the gold, copper and silver mines of the vicinity of Helena, Montana, including the Marysville Mining District, Elliston Mining District, Rimini Mining District, Helena Mining District, Clancy Mining District, Wickes Mining District, Boulder and Basin Mining Districts and the Elkhorn Mining District. Some of the topics include the early history of gold, silver and copper mining in the Helena area, insight into the geology of its mining areas, the local distribution of gold, silver and copper ores, as well their composition and how to identify them. Also included are detailed facts, history, geology and locations of over one hundred gold, silver and copper mines in the area . 8.5" X 11", 162 ppgs, Retail Price: $14.99

Mines and Geology of the Garnet Range of Montana - This important publication on Montana Mining has not been available for over a century. Included are rare insights into the gold, copper and silver mines of the vicinity of this important mining area of Montana. Some of the topics include the early history of gold, silver and copper mining in the Garnet Mountains, insight into the geology of its mining areas, the local distribution of gold, silver and copper ores, as well their composition and how to identify them. Also included are detailed facts, history, geology and locations of numerous gold, silver and copper mines in the area . 8.5" X 11", 100 ppgs, Retail Price: $11.99

Mines and Geology of the Philipsburg Quadrangle of Montana - This important publication on Montana Mining has not been available for over a century. Included are rare insights into the gold, copper and silver mines of the vicinity of this important mining area of Montana. Some of the topics include the early history of gold, silver and copper mining in the Philipsburg Quadrangle, insight into the geology of its mining areas, the local distribution of gold, silver and copper ores, as well their composition and how to identify them. Also included are detailed facts, history, geology and locations of over one hundred gold, silver and copper mines in the area 8.5" X 11", 290 ppgs, Retail Price: $24.99

Geology of the Marysville Mining District of Montana - Included are rare insights into the mining geology of the Marysville Mining District. Some of the topics include the early history of gold, silver and copper mining in the area, insight into the geology of its mining areas, the local distribution of gold, silver and copper ores, as well their composition and how to identify them. Also included are detailed facts, history, geology and locations of gold, silver and copper mines in the area 8.5" X 11", 198 ppgs, Retail Price: $19.99

The Geology and Mines of Northern Idaho and North Western Montana

See listing under Idaho.

Nevada Mining Books

The Bull Frog Mining District of Nevada - Unavailable since 1910, this publication was originally compiled by the United States Department of Interior. This volume also includes important insights into the geologic formations, faults and other aspects of economic geology in this Nevada mining district. Of particular interest are the fine details on many mines in the area, including their locations, histories, development and mineralization. Some of the mines featured include the National Bank Mine, Providence, Gibraltor, Tramps, Denver, Original Bullfrog, Gold Bar, Mayflower, Homestake-King and other mines and prospects. 8.5" X 11", 152 ppgs, Retail Price: $14.99

Colorado Mining Books

Ores of The Leadville Mining District - Unavailable since 1926, this publication was originally compiled by the United States Department of Interior. This volume also includes important insights into the ores and mineralization of the Leadville Mining District in Colorado. Topics include historic ore prospecting methods, local geology, insights into ore veins and stockworks, the local trend and distribution of ore channels, reverse faults, shattered rock above replacement ore bodies, mineral enrichment in oxidized and sulphide zones and more. 8.5" X 11", 66 ppgs, Retail Price: $8.99

Mining in Colorado - Unavailable since 1926, this publication was originally compiled by the United States Department of Interior. This volume also includes important insights into the mining history of Colorado from its early beginnings in the 1850's right up to the mid 1920's. Not only is Colorado's gold mining heritage included, but also its silver, copper, lead and zinc mining industry. Each mining area is treated separately, detailing the development of Colorado's mines on a county by county basis. 8.5" X 11", 284 ppgs, Retail Price: $19.99

Washington Mining Books

The Republic Mining District of Washington - Unavailable since 1910, this important publication was originally published by the Washington Geologic Survey and has been unavailable for a century. Topics include the geology, rock formations and the formation of ore deposits in this important mining area of Washington State. Also included are hard to find details on the geology, history and locations of dozens of mines in the area. Some of the mines featured include the New Republic Mine, Ben Hur, Morning Glory, the South Republic Mine, Quilp, Surprise, Black Tail, Lone Pine, San Poil, Mountain Lion, Tom Thumb, Elcaliph and many others. **8.5" X 11", 94 ppgs, Retail Price: $10.99**

Wyoming Mining Books

Mining in the Laramie Basin of Wyoming - Unavailable since 1909, this publication was originally compiled by the United States Department of Interior. Also included are insights into the mineralization and other characteristics of this important mining region, especially in regards to coal, limestone, gypsum, bentonite clay, cement, sand, clay and copper. **8.5" X 11", 104 ppgs, Retail Price: $11.99**

More Mining Books

Prospecting and Developing A Small Mine - Topics covered include the classification of varying ores, how to take a proper ore sample, the proper reduction of ore samples, alluvial sampling, how to understand geology as it is applied to prospecting and mining, prospecting procedures, methods of ore treatment, the application of drilling and blasting in a small mine and other topics that the small scale miner will find of benefit. **8.5" X 11", 112 ppgs, Retail Price: $11.99**

Timbering For Small Underground Mines - Topics covered include the selection of caps and posts, the treatment of mine timbers, how to install mine timbers, repairing damaged timbers, use of drift supports, headboards, squeeze sets, ore chute construction, mine cribbing, square set timbering methods, the use of steel and concrete sets and other topics that the small underground miner will find of benefit. This volume also includes twenty eight illustrations depicting the proper construction of mine timbering and support systems that greatly enhance the practical usability of the information contained in this small book. **8.5" X 11", 88 ppgs. Retail Price: $10.99**

Timbering and Mining - A classic mining publication on Hard Rock Mining by W.H. Storms. Unavailable since 1909, this rare publication provides an in depth look at American methods of underground mine timbering and mining methods. Topics include the selection and preservation of mine timbers, drifting and drift sets, driving in running ground, structural steel in mine workings, timbering drifts in gravel mines, timbering methods for driving shafts, positioning drill holes in shafts, timbering stations at shafts, drainage, mining large ore bodies by means of open cuts or by the "Glory Hole" system, stoping out ore in flat or low lying veins, use of the "Caving System", stoping in swelling ground, how to stope out large ore bodies, Square Set timbering on the Comstock and its modifications by California miners, the construction of ore chutes, stoping ore bodies by use of the "Block System", how to work dangerous ground, information on the "Delprat System" of stoping without mine timbers, construction and use of headframes and much more. This volume provides a reference into not only practical methods of mining and timbering that may be employed in narrow vein mining by small miners today, but also rare insights into how mines were being worked at the turn of the 19th Century. **8.5" X 11", 288 ppgs. Retail Price: $24.99**

A Study of Ore Deposits For The Practical Miner - Mining historian Kerby Jackson introduces us to a classic mining publication on ore deposits by J.P. Wallace. First published in 1908, it has been unavailable for over a century. Included are important insights into the properties of minerals and their identification, on the occurrence and origin of gold, on gold alloys, insights into gold bearing sulfides such as pyrites and arsenopyrites, on gold bearing vanadium, gold and silver tellurides, lead and mercury tellurides, on silver ores, platinum and iridium, mercury ores, copper ores, lead ores, zinc ores, iron ores, chromium ores, manganese ores, nickel ores, tin ores, tungsten ores and others. Also included are facts regarding rock forming minerals, their composition and occurrences, on igneous, sedimentary, metamorphic and intrusive rocks, as well as how they are geologically disturbed by dikes, flows and faults, as well as the effects of these geologic actions and why they are important to the miner. Written specifically with the common miner and prospector in mind, the book will help to unlock the earth's hidden wealth for you and is written in a simple and concise language that anyone can understand. **8.5" X 11", 366 ppgs. Retail Price: $24.99**

Mine Drainage - Unavailable since 1896, this rare publication provides an in depth look at American methods of underground mine drainage and mining pump systems. This volume provides a reference into not only practical methods of mining drainage that may be employed in narrow vein mining by small miners today, but also rare insights into how mines were being worked at the turn of the 19th Century. **8.5" X 11", 218 ppgs. Retail Price: $24.99**

Fire Assaying Gold, Silver and Lead Ores - Unavailable since 1907, this important publication was originally published by the Mining and Scientific Press and was designed to introduce miners and prospectors of gold, silver and lead to the art of fire assaying. Topics include the fire assaying of ores and products containing gold, silver and lead; the sampling and preparation of ore for an assay; care of the assay office, assay furnaces; crucibles and scorifiers; assay balances; metallic ores; scorification assays; cupelling; parting' crucible assays, the roasting of ores and more. This classic provides a time honored method of assaying put forward in a clear, concise and easy to understand language that will make it a benefit to even beginners. **8.5" X 11", 96 ppgs. Retail Price: $11.99**

Methods of Mine Timbering - Originally published in 1896, this important publication on mining engineering has not been available for nearly a century. Included are rare insights into historical methods of timbering structural support that were used in underground metal mines during the California that still have a practical application for the small scale hardrock miner of today. **8.5" X 11", 94 ppgs. Retail Price: $10.99**

Made in the USA
Monee, IL
04 September 2022